New Directions for
Community Colleges

Arthur M. Cohen
EDITOR-IN-CHIEF

Richard L. Wagoner
ASSOCIATE EDITOR

Gabriel Jones
MANAGING EDITOR

Online
Education

Regina L. Garza Mitchell
EDITOR

LIBRARY
ARAPAHOE COMMUNITY COLLEGE
5900 SOUTH SANTA FE DRIVE
P.O. BOX 9002
LITTLETON, CO 80160-9002

Number 150 • Summer 2010
Jossey-Bass
San Francisco

ONLINE EDUCATION
Regina L. Garza Mitchell (ed.)
New Directions for Community Colleges, no. 150

Arthur M. Cohen, Editor-in-Chief
Richard L. Wagoner, Associate Editor
Gabriel Jones, Managing Editor

Copyright © 2010 Wiley Periodicals, Inc., A Wiley Company. All rights reserved. No part of this publication may be reproduced, stored in a retrieval system, or transmitted in any form or by any means, electronic, mechanical, photocopying, recording, scanning, or otherwise, except as permitted under Section 107 or 108 of the 1976 United States Copyright Act, without either the prior written permission of the Publisher or authorization through payment of the appropriate per-copy fee to the Copyright Clearance Center, 222 Rosewood Drive, Danvers, MA 01923; (978) 750-8400; fax (978) 646-8600. Requests to the Publisher for permission should be addressed to the Permissions Department, c/o John Wiley & Sons, Inc., 111 River St., Hoboken, NJ 07030; (201) 748-8789, fax (201) 748-6326, www.wiley.com/go/permissions.

NEW DIRECTIONS FOR COMMUNITY COLLEGES (ISSN 0194-3081, electronic ISSN 1536-0733) is part of The Jossey-Bass Higher and Adult Education Series and is published quarterly by Wiley Subscription Services, Inc., A Wiley Company, at Jossey-Bass, 989 Market Street, San Francisco, California 94103-1741. Periodicals Postage Paid at San Francisco, California, and at additional mailing offices. POSTMASTER: Send address changes to New Directions for Community Colleges, Jossey-Bass, 989 Market Street, San Francisco, California 94103-1741.

SUBSCRIPTIONS cost $98.00 for individuals and $269.00 for institutions, agencies, and libraries in the United States. Prices subject to change.

EDITORIAL CORRESPONDENCE should be sent to the Editor-in-Chief, Arthur M. Cohen, at the Graduate School of Education and Information Studies, University of California, Box 951521, Los Angeles, California 90095-1521. All manuscripts receive anonymous reviews by external referees.

New Directions for Community Colleges is indexed in CIJE: Current Index to Journals in Education (ERIC), Contents Pages in Education (T&F), Current Abstracts (EBSCO), Ed/Net (Simpson Communications), Education Index/Abstracts (H. W. Wilson), Educational Research Abstracts Online (T&F), ERIC Database (Education Resources Information Center), and Resources in Education (ERIC).

Microfilm copies of issues and articles are available in 16mm and 35mm, as well as microfiche in 105mm, through University Microfilms Inc., 300 North Zeeb Road, Ann Arbor, Michigan 48106-1346.

CONTENTS

EDITOR'S NOTES

Education has undergone vast changes over the past twenty years in response to developments in technology, and these changes have contributed to the rapid integration and evolution of online education in community colleges. Community colleges initially turned to online educational offerings in response to student and public demands and as a means of remaining competitive in the rapidly developing educational marketplace. As technology evolved, so did colleges' ability to offer courses and services electronically. The use of online education has increased steadily since the early 1990s, and community colleges now serve the majority of students enrolled in online courses (Allen and Seaman, 2008). Growth in the number of online course offerings occurred rapidly, resulting in a reactive response to providing this type of education.

The importance of online education was underscored in two earlier volumes of *New Directions for Community Colleges* that addressed issues associated with implementing online education. In 1997, Dillon and Cintrón explored the impact of distance education on policy, and Bower and Hardy followed up in 2004 in an examination of best practices for implementing online education. Both volumes provided a foundation for exploring and addressing immediate issues associated with online education. However, many colleges have moved beyond implementation phases, with future growth in online education and its associated influences of change expected to occur in colleges with existing online course and program offerings (Allen and Seaman, 2007, 2008). Online course offerings and programs have become institutionalized at many colleges, moving areas of interest beyond initial implementation concerns and toward a focus on what is lacking and where improvements can be made.

The integration of technology and education has resulted in ideological and physical adjustments. Although online education initially was assumed to be just another mechanism for instruction, emerging research indicates that its impact goes well beyond the way that courses are offered and has altered both the structure and culture of the community college (Garza Mitchell, 2009; Jones and O'Shea, 2004). With the integration of online education at two-year colleges came visible changes to physical and organizational infrastructures, such as the creation or expansion of distance education departments and mechanisms for course delivery such as learning management systems. Less obvious changes occurred in other areas as well. The principles underlying online instruction stem from constructivist theories (Meyer, 2002), which are important to the way that colleges

New Directions for Community Colleges, no. 150, Summer 2010 © 2010 Wiley Periodicals, Inc.
Published online in Wiley InterScience (www.interscience.wiley.com) • DOI: 10.1002/cc.399

approach teaching and learning both online and face-to-face. In addition, the structure of online education has implications for hiring, financial models, governance, and more (Jones and O'Shea, 2004). For instance, when online courses and degrees are offered, student and academic services must also be provided in electronic formats. Thus, many colleges have moved toward electronic services for all students, not just those who take courses online. This change has had financial implications in terms of sustaining the physical infrastructure, hiring and training faculty, and student tuition revenue. Yet another area of concern is student access (Cejda, 2007; Cox, 2005). Has online education opened doors for those who could not otherwise take courses? What are the implications for rural students with limited Internet access or students who cannot afford state-of-the-art computers?

Community colleges are mission driven, and an examination of online education in this setting would not be complete without an investigation of the intersection between the two. Online education has evolved from external changes associated with globalization and the economy, so it would be easy to presume that values associated with online education reflect those of academic capitalism. While many colleges admit that they hope that online education will increase the number of students, and therefore credit hours, most claim that increasing access is the main reason for offering online courses and programs (Cox, 2005). Therefore, focus must now shift to studying the deeper changes that have occurred as the result of online education and the impact on institutional mission and culture.

Online education is relatively new to higher education, and research is ongoing about its impact on the community college. Online education is highly influenced by external forces such as technology and societal demands, which are in turn reflected institutionally (Moore and Kearsley, 2005). Community colleges have faced numerous changes over the past twenty years, and online education is one of the greatest facilitators of this change. For example, many colleges first offered student services in an online format to attend to the needs of online students. This volume examines changes evoked by the continued adaptation of community colleges to online education, highlighting the reverberating impact on the community college as a whole.

This volume will appeal to community college faculty, staff, and administrators who are directly or indirectly involved with online education and to researchers of community college issues. It will be of interest as well to those concerned with how the community college continues to adapt to external societal, technological, and economic changes.

Growth in community college online education has increased significantly over the past decade. As the need for and popularity of online courses have increased, so have the challenges associated with it. Chapters One and Two set the stage for the volume by discussing current issues. In Chapter One, Brent Cejda reviews relevant research and literature regarding the challenges facing community colleges in the delivery of online courses and programs. In Chapter Two, Jay Leist and Jon Travis focus specifically on challenges that rural community colleges face in delivering online education, highlighting the importance of planning, through examining the efforts of six rural institutions.

Rural colleges in particular rely on online courses and programs to expand their reach. However, they also face greater challenges in securing appropriate resources to run and expand online programs. In Chapter Three, Gwladys Austin reflects on her experiences at a growing rural institution that has greatly expanded its online offerings over the past several years. She describes the challenges, changes, and rewards associated with this program growth.

Chapters Four and Five highlight the changing role of faculty. In Chapter Four, Jeffrey Hoyle describes his journey from novice to experienced adjunct faculty member and the lessons he has learned along the way. Chapter Five expands on the impact of technology on the faculty role as Vernon Smith reports on the skill set that is required when developing and teaching online courses and the resulting transformation in expectations for faculty.

While colleges attempt to adjust to existing technologies, those technologies continue to be updated and enhanced. Over the past three years alone, a vast array of new technologies has become available at little or no cost to institutions (Sclater, 2008). Collectively known as Web 2.0, these tools offer numerous teaching and learning opportunities for faculty, students, and staff. In Chapter Six, Veronica Diaz discusses the possibilities and pitfalls colleges face as they attempt to incorporate this new generation of technology tools into online courses. Jaime Lester and Michael Perini explore in Chapter Seven the potential for colleges to harness one particular aspect of Web 2.0, social networking sites, as a mechanism for increasing student engagement.

Anne Hornak, Kayeri Akweks, and Madeline Jeffs examine in Chapter Eight the changing nature of student services in the online environment. There is now an expectation that various services are available electronically for both online and campus-based students. This chapter highlights the need to continually assess services offered in the online environment.

The word *quality* is often used in conjunction with online education. There is a great push for community colleges to offer quality courses, programs, and services, particularly when the number of online students continues to grow exponentially. In Chapter Nine, I challenge readers to define the notion of quality in online education and consider the idea that quality may be defined differently by each institution.

In Chapter Ten, Albert Lorenzo provides a summary of challenges posed by online education and offers insights into what lies ahead. He explores institutional issues and opportunities in addition to public policy perspectives. He also provides a framework for guiding strategic conversations among planners and practitioners as they work together to chart a future course for their institutions.

Like most other research related to technology, elements of this volume will most likely be outdated by the time it sees print. Yet the lessons provided here will remain invaluable for moving into the next generation of online education with foundational elements in place for building and enhancing quality programs. Research presented in this volume provides information that will help guide us into the next generation of online education by illustrating strengths and weaknesses in approaches to building high quality online programs. Readers can learn what others have done and apply the best practices that work within their college and for their given needs, adding on new approaches based on this past experience. Emerging technologies continue to expand possibilities for teaching and learning and for the use of technology in serving online students. The challenge for colleges remains in keeping up with the rapid pace of technological evolution and using technology for the betterment of online education as opposed to using technology for its own sake. The intention of this volume is to provide direction in solving some of the problems that have plagued colleges since they first offered online courses more than ten years ago by generating conversation around issues that many are either not aware of or choose to ignore.

Regina L. Garza Mitchell
Editor

References

Allen, I. E., and Seaman, J. *Online Nation: Five Years of Growth in Online Learning.* Needham, Mass.: Sloan Consortium, 2007.
Allen, I. E., and Seaman, J. *Staying the Course: Online Education in the United States, 2008.* Needham, Mass.: Sloan Consortium, 2008.
Bower, B. L., & Hardy, K. P. *From Distance Education to E-Learning: Lessons Along the Way, New Directions for Community Colleges 128.* San Francisco, CA: Jossey-Bass, 2004.
Cejda, B. D. "Connecting to the Larger World: Distance Education in Rural Community Colleges." In P. L. Eddy and J. P. Murray (eds.), *Rural Community Colleges: Teaching, Learning, and Leading in the Heartland.* New Directions for Community Colleges, no. 137. San Francisco: Jossey-Bass, 2007.
Cox, R. D. "Online Education as Institutional Myth: Rituals and Realities at Community Colleges." *Teachers College Record,* 2005, *107*(8), 1754-1787.
Dillon, C. L., & Cintrón, R. *Building a Working Policy for Distance Education, New Directions for Community Colleges 99.* San Francisco, CA: Jossey-Bass, 1997.
Garza Mitchell, R. L. "Online Education and Organizational Change." *Community College Review,* 2009, *37*(1), 81-101.
Jones, N., and O'Shea, J. "Challenging Hierarchies: The Impact of E-Learning." *Higher Education,* 2004, *48*(3), 379-395.
Meyer, K. A. *Quality in Distance Education: Focus on Online Learning.* ASHE-ERIC Higher Education Report Series, *29*(4). San Francisco: Jossey-Bass, 2002.

Moore, M. G., and Kearsley, G. *Distance Education: A Systems View.* (2nd ed.) Belmont, Calif.: Thomson/Wadsworth, 2005.
Sclater, N. *Web 2.0, Personal Learning Environments, and the Future of Learning Management Systems.* Boulder, Colo.: EDUCAUSE Center for Applied Research, 2008.

REGINA L. GARZA MITCHELL is assistant professor of educational leadership at Central Michigan University in Mount Pleasant, Michigan. She was previously director of distance education for a medium-sized rural community college.

This chapter explores the tremendous growth in the use of the Internet to deliver distance education at community colleges. The author examines various definitions of online education, including the types of courses, programs, and degrees available and the types of community colleges that offer greater amounts of online programming. Considerations for the future growth of online education are provided.

Online Education in Community Colleges

Brent Cejda

In the past decade, distance education has become synonymous with the Internet. Kinley (2001) noted that "today's distance education focus has dramatically shifted toward network-based technologies (in general) and Internet-based delivery (more specifically)" (p. 7). With a reputation for adaptability, community colleges would seem likely to lead the way in online education. Data from the National Center for Education Statistics (NCES) support this assumption. In the 2006–2007 academic year, 96 percent of public community colleges offered at least once course online, compared to 86 percent of public four-year institutions (Parsad and Lewis, 2008). Allen and Seaman (2008) stress, however, that the impact of online education is much greater at community colleges, as 37 percent of the total student population attends a community college, over 50 percent of all online enrollments are at two-year institutions.

The Emergence of Online Education at Community Colleges

The dominance of Internet delivery among distance education technologies used by public community colleges is displayed in Table 1.1. What is not shown in the table is the shift to the Internet as the predominant method to deliver instruction. In 2000–2001, 60 percent of public community colleges reported using two-way audiovisual technology for distance delivery, and 57 percent reported using one-way prerecorded video (Waits and Lewis, 2003). These data support Allen and Seaman's (2007) finding: community colleges that offered courses over the Internet in 2000 have dramatically

New Directions for Community Colleges, no. 150, Summer 2010 © 2010 Wiley Periodicals, Inc.
Published online in Wiley InterScience (www.interscience.wiley.com) • DOI: 10.1002/cc.400

7

Table 1.1.   Distance Education Technologies Used at Community Colleges

Primary Technology for Instructional Delivery	Percentage Using
Asynchronous Internet	93
Two-way audiovisual	30
Synchronous Internet	28
One-way prerecorded video	21
Correspondence with technology	11
One-way audio	10
Correspondence only	9
One-way video/two-way audio	8
Other technologies	4

Source: U.S. Department of Education (2007).

increased the number of online offerings and dramatically decreased the number of offerings using other technologies.

Recognizing the need to gather information concerning the use of Internet delivery in higher education, the Sloan Consortium began an annual survey of online education in 2003 (Allen and Seaman, 2003). The consortium reports do not present longitudinal data on the same specific factors, but the fifth survey provided a summary of online growth at community colleges over the previous years. Allen and Seaman (2007) found that institutions classified by the Carnegie Foundation as Associate's Colleges experienced the greatest increases in online enrollments, from slightly more than 800,000 students in fall 2002 to slightly more than 1.9 million students in fall 2006. In fact, more students were enrolled in online courses at community colleges in fall 2006 than in all other types of institutions combined.

The Instructional Technology Council (ITC), an affiliate council of the American Association of Community Colleges (AACC), initiated an annual survey of distance education in 2005 (Lokken, 2009). ITC administered the survey to its members the first year and then revised the instrument and distributed the survey to its membership and AACC members in subsequent years. Responding institutions reported growth in online enrollments of 15 percent from fall 2004 to fall 2005, 18 percent from fall 2005 to fall 2006, and 11 percent from fall 2006 to fall 2007 (Instructional Technology Council, 2006; Lokken, 2009; Lokken and Womer, 2007). Because the increase in online enrollments is substantially greater than the overall enrollment growth, Lokken (2009) contends that online programs have "become THE primary source for enrollment growth" in community colleges (p. 9).

Defining *Online*

Examining the literature regarding online education is difficult because of the lack of a universal definition. The 2008 Higher Education Opportunity

Table 1.2. Definition Used to Designate a Course as Online at Community Colleges

Minimum Percentage of Online Instruction Used to Designate Course as Online	Percentage
100 percent	63
80 to 99 percent	12
50 to 79 percent	11
25 to 49 percent	5
Other criterion used to designate online	5
No standard criterion used to designate online	4

Source: U.S. Department of Education (2007).

Act includes the Internet as one of the technologies used in the definition of *distance education* but does not provide any definition of exactly what constitutes a course delivered over the Internet. The Sloan Consortium classifies an online course as one with 80 percent or more of its content delivered online and, typically, having no face-to-face meetings (Allen and Seaman, 2003), and it has used that description in each of its annual surveys.

Table 1.2 presents data, gathered by the U.S. Department of Education's National Center for Educational Statistics, indicating the wide variance in the percentage of online instruction used to designate a course as online. As shown in the table, 25 percent of public community colleges do not use the 80 percent criterion established in the Sloan typology, which may lead to discrepancies in reporting about online classes.

There are also discrepancies in determining exactly what constitutes an online program. The ITC definition of an online program is one where "at least 70 percent of coursework needed to complete the degree is available online" (Lokken and Womer, 2007, p. 5). When the 70 percent threshold is used, 74 percent of the institutions responding to the most recent survey indicate that they offer at least one online degree (Lokken, 2009). A previous Sloan survey found that in fall 2005, 31.2 percent of associate institutions offered programs that were totally available online (Allen and Seaman, 2006).

Part of the difficulty in determining what constitutes an online course or a complete online program or degree lies in the fact that many community colleges involved in distance education are not alone in their effort. Participation in a distance education consortium is reported by 83 percent of public two-year institutions (Waits and Lewis, 2003). Most community colleges participated in a state (87 percent) or system or district (49 percent) consortium. Less common are regional (9 percent), national (6 percent), and international (2 percent) consortia. The following two examples illustrate some of the dilemmas posed in reporting online courses and programs.

NEW DIRECTIONS FOR COMMUNITY COLLEGES • DOI: 10.1002/cc

WashingtonOnline (WAOL), a program under the management of the Washington State Board of Technical and Community Colleges, was created to provide students the opportunity to complete an online associate of arts degree. Broughton (2009) described three types of online courses that the program tracks:

1. Shared courses that are system owned were developed using resources from thirty-three technical and community colleges. Any of these institutions can offer a system-owned shared course. In addition, there are times when students from multiple institutions enroll in one offering (combining fewer numbers of students from the respective institutions to enable a sufficient enrollment for a course to make).
2. Shared courses that are college owned were developed using resources of one technical or community college. Students from other institutions are allowed to enroll in the course through WAOL.
3. Private courses are offered only by the respective technical or community college, and only students from that institution are allowed to enroll in the course.

One of the more recent reports (Washington State Board, 2004) identifies 3,411 shared courses that were system owned, 569 courses that were college owned, and 2,141 private courses. Twenty-eight institutions reported offering a shared course that was system owned. If all of these institutions offered the same course (for example, college algebra), is it best described as twenty-eight courses or twenty-eight sections of the one course? If students from multiple institutions are in the same course, enrolled through WAOL, does each institution indicate that it offered the class? These questions are not meant as criticism of the program or the reporting procedures of WAOL. Rather, the example is used to illustrate the difficulty of identifying and reporting courses, sections of courses, and designation of the offering institution.

A study of distance education in rural community colleges (Cejda, 2007) illustrates the difficulty in identifying an online program or degree. None of the 114 responding institutions indicated that they provided a degree program that could be completed totally online. When online offerings available through formal consortia or transfer agreements are added, however, 51 percent of the responding institutions indicated that at least one degree could be completed entirely online. And if all forms of distance technologies were included, slightly more than four-fifths (81 percent) of the institutions indicated that students could complete a degree. This example illustrates that the responding institutions perceived that a fully online degree option meant their own institution offered all of the courses in that format. Other institutions may perceive that any online course from any institution would fit either the ITC or Sloan definition of an online degree. Moreover, there appears to be a need to define a blended or hybrid online degree that combines a designated percentage of online courses and a designated percentage of courses delivered using other distance technologies.

Online Offerings

Community colleges offer a wide breadth of courses and programs (academic transfer, vocational, English as a Second Language, developmental, credit, and noncredit, for example) and a variety of credentials and degrees (certificates, associate of arts, associate of science, associate of applied science, and associate of general studies, and, more recently, bachelor of art and bachelor of science). In addition, the Carnegie Foundation now classifies community colleges by geographical location (rural, suburban, urban) and enrollment (small, medium, large). This section focuses on the literature that addresses differences in online offerings by course or program area or differences among community colleges with respect to geographical location or size.

The most recent ITC survey (Lokken, 2009) found that 64 percent of the responding institutions offered noncredit online courses. This is a 3 percent decline from the previous year, and the economic downturn is cited as a possible reason. A comprehensive literature review did not reveal any additional sources that provided data concerning noncredit online offerings. Moreover, the literature review did not identify any sources focused on online English as a Second Language or developmental education programs.

Johnson and others (2004) examined distance offerings in career and technical education (CTE) using a random sample of 512 member institutions of the AACC. The authors did not provide a specific definition of CTE, explaining that the term includes both credit and noncredit offerings and ranges from a single course providing specific skill training to certificates and associate of applied science degrees. Information was gathered using AACC categories of urban, suburban or large town, and rural, but no definition of these categories is provided in the article. Responses were received from 270 institutions (53 percent). Within the responding institutions, 76.3 percent offered CTE courses using distance technologies in 2000–2001. In terms of online CTE credit offerings, the percentages for rural community colleges percentages are slightly lower (71.9 percent) than for urban (74.3 percent) and suburban (78.7 percent) community colleges. Rural community colleges, however, offered a slightly higher percentage (48.4 percent) of online noncredit CTE courses than did their urban counterparts (43.7 percent) and almost the same percentage as suburban (50 percent) institutions.

Cejda (2007) collected data on the online academic transfer and vocational offerings of rural community colleges in nine states: Arkansas, Arizona, Colorado, Louisiana, New Mexico, Oklahoma, Texas, Utah, and Wyoming. From the population of 202 public two-year institutions in these

**Table 1.3.   Percentage of Associate Degrees Offered
Through Online Programs**

Degree	2008	2007	2006
Associate of arts	76	45	48
Associate of science	40	28	37
Associate of applied science	43	25	32
Associate of general studies	10	6	7

Note: Online degrees are defined as "at least 70 percent of coursework needed to complete the degree is available online."
Sources: Instructional Technology Council (2006, 2007, 2009).

states, 114 usable returns were received, a 56 percent return rate. Using the scheme developed by Katsinas (2003), 73 (64 percent) of the usable returns were from institutions classified as rural and 69 (95 percent) used the Internet to deliver courses. Respondents indicated that their institutions offered more online academic transfer courses in comparison to vocational courses. Slightly more than the majority (51 percent) of rural community colleges in these states indicated that at least one academic transfer degree could be completed totally online using consortia and transfer agreements. Only two institutions (3 percent) indicated that a vocational degree could be earned completely through online instruction. The format of the survey did not gather information on whether certificate or other preassociate degree credentials in vocational areas could be completed through online courses.

Table 1.3 presents information from the ITC surveys regarding the types of associate degrees offered through online programs. Results from the most recent survey (Lokken, 2009) reveal a 10 percent increase in the number of institutions that offer an online degree, from 64 percent in 2007 to 74 percent in 2008. The review of literature did not identify any information on the number of community colleges that offer multiple types of online degrees.

As a means of examining online offerings by disciplinary areas, the Sloan survey identified eight subject areas in which the greatest number of degrees had been awarded (Allen and Seaman, 2008): business; liberal arts and sciences, general studies, and humanities; health professions and related sciences; education; computer and information sciences; social sciences and history; psychology; and engineering. Institutions were then asked to indicate if they had fully online programs in these disciplinary areas, and an "online penetration" rate was calculated, using "the ratio of the number of institutions offering a fully online program in that discipline to those offering that program using any delivery mechanism" (p. 13). In comparison to doctoral/research, master's, baccalaureate, and specialized institutions, associate institutions have a higher penetration rate in five of the eight disciplines: psychology; social sciences and history; computer and information sciences; liberal arts and sciences, general studies, and humanities; and business.

Data from the U.S. Department of Education (Parsad and Lewis, 2008) indicate a relationship between institutional size and the number of online offerings. Less than half (46 percent) of the institutions with an enrollment of three thousand or fewer students reported offering online courses, compared to 95 percent of the institutions with an enrollment of ten thousand or more students. Reports from the Sloan Consortium (Allen and Seaman, 2006, 2008) point to a strong relationship between institutional enrollment and the extent of online offerings. Institutions with larger enrollments were among the first to begin online offerings and are more like to offer a fully online degree. Although both of these sources have two- and four-year institutions in their analysis, the data also point to the question of whether a relationship exists between the size of a community college and its participation in a consortium.

With the shift of distance technology to online delivery, a disparity of Internet use by geographical region became a concern. Sink and Jackson (2000) were among the first to identify a digital divide between urban and rural community colleges. This divide existed in the institutional infrastructure and, in part, explains why some rural community colleges developed online offerings later than those in suburban or urban settings. Katsinas and Moeck (2002), however, argued that technological advancements leading to high-speed or broadband connections in the home were actually widening the digital divide. A recent report (Horrigan, 2008) indicates that home broadband connection in rural America increased by 23 percent from 2007 to 2008. But even with this gain, broadband connection in rural homes lags 19 percent behind that of urban homes and 22 percent behind that of suburban homes. The review of the literature did not identify any studies that addressed the implications of limited broadband access in rural locations on participation in online education programs.

The Future of Online Programs

Allen and Seaman (2008) point out that the vast majority of growth in online enrollments came first through the number of institutions that added online offerings and then through the expansion of existing programs. As a result, institutions that have not yet ventured into online education are those that have the smallest enrollments. How much more enrollment growth can be expected in online programs? Can enrollment numbers be maintained?

Gallagher (2002) points out that community colleges have made significant efforts to provide academic support for students, so they are more likely to have the capacity to provide this support using distance technologies. But community colleges may not have as great a capacity for providing professional development for faculty or student services through distance technologies. A comprehensive evaluation of the capacity of the institution in regard to the platform used to deliver instruction, student and faculty support, technology infrastructure, and program administration must be undertaken, and the necessary steps to provide capacity in these areas must be developed for additional growth to occur and to sustain existing programming.

Capacity is not a term specifically used, but the concept appears frequently in the literature concerning online education. Having an adequate support staff to provide training and technical assistance, providing adequate student services for distance education students, and operating and equipment budgets have been ranked as the top three concerns of program administrators at community colleges (Lokken, 2009). Providing training and technical assistance also appears to be a key component in gaining faculty acceptance of online education (O'Quinn and Corry, 2002; Roberson and Klotz, 2002). Having faculty capacity to meet the demand for online courses and programs appears to be a growing concern. In both the 2007 and 2008 ITC surveys, 69 percent of the respondents indicated that their community college was not meeting the student demand for online offerings (Lokken, 2009).

The faculty members who teach online courses in part drive the concern of faculty capacity. Institutions responding to the ITC survey indicate that 67 percent of online courses are taught by full-time faculty (Lokken and Womer, 2007). This finding is consistent with the Sloan survey, where slightly more than two-thirds (68 percent) of associate-classified institutions report that their online classes are taught primarily by full-time faculty members (Allen and Seaman, 2005). If online courses are predominantly taught by full-time faculty and community colleges continue to rely heavily on adjuncts, the continued growth of online enrollments is questionable. Lokken (2009) found workload issues to be the greatest challenge about working with faculty that online administrators reported.

The vast majority of community colleges have successfully implemented online offerings, and many have experienced substantial enrollment growth through online programs. Lokken (2009) describes the typical online program as "under-staffed, working in cramped conditions, with an inadequate budget" (p. 9). With community colleges in most states experiencing funding concerns, the primary suggestions for practitioners are to adopt the following definitions and reporting standards:

- The Sloan Consortium standard of an online course consisting of 80 percent or greater of the content delivered online and having no face-to-face meetings
- The ITC standard of an online program providing a minimum of 70 percent of the course work needed to complete the degree available online

NEW DIRECTIONS FOR COMMUNITY COLLEGES • DOI: 10.1002/cc

- Classification of courses, degrees and enrollment as institutional (offered by and available only to students at a particular institution), consortium based (offered through a formal partnership or agreement), or visiting (enrollment allowed to a guest or visiting student).

Establishing consensus about definitions regarding online courses, online degrees, and developing common reporting standards of enrollment is necessary to sustain current programming and justify funding to implement additional offerings.

References

Allen, I. E., and Seaman, J. *Sizing the Opportunity: The Quality and Extent of Online Education in the United States, 2002 and 2003.* Needham, Mass.: Sloan Consortium, 2003.

Allen, I. E., and Seaman, J. *Growing by Degrees: Online Education in the United States, 2005.* Needham, Mass.: Sloan Consortium, 2005.

Allen, I. E., and Seaman, J. *Making the Grade: Online Education in the United States, 2006.* Needham, Mass.: Sloan Consortium, 2006.

Allen, I. E., and Seaman, J. *Online Nation: Five Years of Growth in Online Learning.* Needham, Mass.: Sloan Consortium, 2007.

Allen, I. E., and Seaman, J. *Staying the Course: Online Education in the United States, 2008.* Needham, Mass.: Sloan Consortium, 2008.

Broughton (personal communication, July 11, 2009)

Cejda, B. D. "Distance Education in Rural Community Colleges." *Community College Journal of Research and Practice,* 2007, *31,* 291-230.

Gallagher, S. *Distance Learning at the Tipping point: Critical Success Factors to Growing Fully Online Distance Learning Programs.* Boston: Eduventures, 2002.

Higher Education Opportunity Act. Public Law 110-315 enacted on August 14, 2008. Retrieved on March 12, 2009 from http://www.ed.gov/policy/highered/leg/hea08/index.html

Horrigan, J. B. *Home Broadband Adoption 2008.* Washington, D.C.: Pew Internet and American Life Project, 2008. Retrieved Mar. 12, 2009, from http://www.pewinternet.org/.

Instructional Technology Council. *ITC Second Annual Survey on Distance Education.* Washington, D.C.: Instructional Technology Council, 2006.

Johnson, S. D., and others. "Internet-Based Learning in Postsecondary Career and Technical Education." *Journal of Vocational Education Research,* 2004, *29*(2), 101-120. Retrieved Jan. 7, 2009, from http://scholar.lib.vt.edu/ejournals/JVER/.

Katsinas, S. G. "Two-Year College Classifications Based on Institutional Control, Geography, Governance, and Size." In A. C. McCormick and R. D. Cox (eds.), *Classification Systems for Community Colleges.* New Directions for Community Colleges, no. 122. San Francisco: Jossey-Bass, 2003.

Katsinas, S. G., & Moeck, P. "The Digital Divide and Rural Community Colleges: Problems and Prospects." *Community College Journal of Research and Practice,* 2002, *26*(3), 207-224.

Kinley, E. R. "Implementing Distance Education, the Impact of Institutional Characteristics: A View from the Department Chair's Chair." Unpublished doctoral dissertation, University of Nebraska-Lincoln, 2001.

Lokken, F. *2008 Distance Education Survey Results: Tracking the Impact of eLearning at Community Colleges.* Washington, D.C.: Instructional Technology Council, 2009.

Lokken, F., and Womer, L. *Trends in e-Learning: Tracking the Impact of e-Learning in Higher Education.* Washington, D.C.: Instructional Technology Council, 2007.

O'Quinn, L., and Corry, M. "Factors That Deter Faculty from Participating in Distance Education." *Journal of Distance Learning Administration,* 2002, 5(4), 1-18. Retrieved Jan. 7, 2009, from ww.westga.edu/~distance/ jmain11.html.

Parsad, B., and Lewis, L. *Distance Education at Degree-Granting Postsecondary Institutions: 2006-07.* Washington, D.C.: National Center for Education Statistics, 2008.

Roberson, T. J., and Klotz, J. "How Can Instructors and Administrators Fill the Missing Link in Online Instruction?" *Journal of Distance Learning Administration,* 2002, 5(4), 1-7. Retrieved Mar. 12, 2009, from www.westga.edu/~distance/jmain11.html.

Sink, D. W., and Jackson, K. L. "Bridging the Digital Divide: A Collaborative Approach." *Community College Journal,* 2000, 71(2), 38-41.

U.S. Department of Education, National Center for Education Statistics. "Distance Education at Postsecondary Institutions." Washington, D.C.: U.S. Government Printing Office, 2007.

Waits, T., and Lewis, L. *Distance Education at Degree-Granting Postsecondary Institutions: 2000–2001.* Washington, D.C.: U.S. Government Printing Office, 2003.

Washington State Board of Technical and Community Colleges. "WashingtonOnline 2004 Enrollment Report." Retrieved July 11, 2009, from www.sbctc.ctc.edu/college/delearning.aspx.

BRENT CEJDA *is an associate professor in the educational leadership and higher education program at the University of Nebraska-Lincoln.*

NEW DIRECTIONS FOR COMMUNITY COLLEGES • DOI: 10.1002/cc

2

Rural community colleges often expand their online course offerings in an ad hoc manner. Due to limited resources and competing priorities, the necessary, careful planning for online instruction is often forgotten.

Planning for Online Courses at Rural Community Colleges

Jay Leist, Jon Travis

The delivery of courses and even complete degree programs online has become commonplace in higher education. As institutions seek to extend their reach and students demand more convenient access to the college curriculum, online offerings have increased at an accelerating rate. What has not kept pace with this expansion of online offerings is the necessary corresponding development of planning to ensure that quality is incorporated with the increase in online delivery (Bathe, 2001). Although comparisons of online and face-to-face instruction have not shown a difference in quality (Allen and Seaman, 2006), a lack of planning for online instruction can reduce its effectiveness.

This chapter examines the value of online instruction to rural community colleges, the importance of planning for these courses, and the actual planning that selected rural community colleges have undertaken. As this examination demonstrates, online course planning, as vital as it is to rural campuses, is often overlooked as colleges rush to jump on the fast-moving train of online instruction.

Online Courses and Rural Community Colleges: Benefits and Challenges

Like their urban and suburban counterparts, many rural community colleges have incorporated online courses into degree and certificate programs

NEW DIRECTIONS FOR COMMUNITY COLLEGES, no. 150, Summer 2010 © 2010 Wiley Periodicals, Inc.
Published online in Wiley InterScience (www.interscience.wiley.com) • DOI: 10.1002/cc.401

to improve their educational reach. Distance education has provided a way to communicate with individuals dispersed over large geographical expanses, and no other sector of higher education is more affected by geography than rural community colleges. With many colleges located in sparsely populated locales, the service areas of these institutions typically span multiple counties and thousands of square miles. Increased technology, often in the form of online courses, has great potential for delivering courses to even the most isolated reaches of the nation.

Online courses also offer a level of economic convenience for these institutions and their students. The remoteness of many rural community colleges usually translates into small enrollments, with a correspondingly small number of full- and part-time faculty members. Online courses offer the potential to maximize instructional assets. Such courses "eliminate the classroom walls that restrict class size and . . . have the potential to enroll large numbers of students" (Mupinga and Maughan, 2008, p. 17). Students in rural areas can also profit from the flexibility and convenience of online courses, which can greatly reduce or even eliminate long commutes for a face-to-face class, thus saving time and the costs associated with high gasoline prices.

Despite holding great potential for improving educational reach, and therefore enhancing student enrollments, online courses pose at least three major resource challenges for many rural community colleges: fiscal issues, a shortage of faculty and staff members, and digital divide concerns. Many rural areas face high rates of unemployment and illiteracy and low educational attainment levels. These characteristics can have a profound impact on a local tax base and result in the lack of funds for expensive curricular programs, faculty salaries, and professional development (Murray, 2007).

This lack of funding often results in a shortage of full-time faculty and staff to develop and deliver quality online courses. Murray (2007) noted that a rural faculty member often functions as the only instructor for a given discipline. Hence, these faculty members are often reluctant to participate in any form of distance education (Cejda, 2007). This reluctance is frequently exacerbated by a lack of technology support staff, who are essential to the development and delivery of online courses. Unfortunately, many rural community colleges lack this capacity because their support staffs wear too many hats.

No discussion about rural community colleges and the challenges presented by online instruction would be complete without mentioning the digital divide. As early as 2000, Sink and Jackson used this term to describe a technological gap in which urban community colleges typically enjoy better connectivity than rural institutions. As used here, *connectivity* means the level of "quality and reliability of the connection for access to the Internet" (Page and Hill, 2008, p. 68). Connectivity issues (posed, for example, by the availability of only dial-up Internet service) place rural colleges and their students at a disadvantage for maximizing the use of

NEW DIRECTIONS FOR COMMUNITY COLLEGES • DOI: 10.1002/cc

technological resources (Cejda, 2007). To deal effectively with these issues, rural community colleges must commit to serious, deliberate planning for online courses.

What the Literature Says About Planning for Online Courses

In 1989, the League for Innovation in the Community College published *Planning Guide for Instructional Computing Resources*. The guide addressed issues of resources and support, environmental assessment, staff development, and planning. As institutions acquired hardware and software in the 1980s, many did so in an ad hoc manner, often overlooking such important concerns as standards and interconnectivity, infrastructure, training, and obsolescence. Some two-year college districts, however, recognized the need for planning and managing the ever-growing inventory of technology. The Maricopa Community College District in Arizona, for example, developed a technology planning and management task force, called Ocotillo, in the late 1980s (Travis, 1992). The College and University System Exchange (CAUSE), which eventually became EDUCAUSE, began as a collaboration to address similar concerns. With the publication of *The Learning Action Plan: A New Approach to Information Technology Planning in Community Colleges* (Baltzer, 1994), CAUSE provided a useful follow-up to the league's monograph.

More recently, Pisel (2008) pointed to systematic strategic planning as a way to improve the likelihood of success for distance education programs, especially when institutions are concerned with the long-term commitment of resources. He also noted that within higher education, strategic planning is seldom done well. Typically planning that does occur emphasizes lower-level concerns.

Whether their efforts rise to a strategic level, rural community colleges can benefit by planning for online courses. At a minimum, this planning should consider four key areas: network maintenance, faculty compensation, training and professional development, and assessment. Maintenance of the network infrastructure (who will perform it) requires in-depth planning (Downey, 2001). Although in-house technology staff can usually maintain small- and medium-sized networks, planning may determine that greater benefits exist by contracting with an outside agency for system repairs and upgrades. Compensation for instructors involved with online courses also warrants planning. In their examination of online courses and community college faculty workloads, Mupinga and Maughan (2008) reaffirmed what has become common knowledge throughout higher education: "Web-based courses require more time and effort . . . compared with traditional face-to-face courses" (p. 17). Common forms of compensation include limitations for online course loads, release time, and monetary incentives.

Training and professional development serve as cornerstones of online programs. Although they merit in-depth planning, these areas do not always receive enough attention. Mupinga and Maughan (2008) noted that approximately 40 percent of higher education institutions offering distance education courses ask instructors to teach these classes "without providing [these instructors with] any special preparation" (p. 18). Given the change in instructional culture required for online teaching, faculty need some kind of training to augment their existing skills (Travis and Price, 2005). Assessment is another crucial planning consideration to ensure quality online instructional programs. Downey (2001) suggested three key areas for assessing online instructional programs: student learning gains, usability and versatility, and financial viability.

From the Field: Online Courses at Six Rural Community Colleges

Although in-depth planning has the potential to enhance an online instructional program, it requires the commitment of time, money, and personnel—resources in short supply at many rural community colleges. Because these colleges seldom have adequate resources to support an institutional planning office, this function frequently becomes another hat that administrators, instructors, and staff members must wear.

These issues led us to examine the planning efforts and program activities of online instructional programs at six public rural community colleges in a southwestern state. In-depth telephone interviews with the self-identified distance learning administrator (DLA) served as the method for data collection. At two of the colleges, the chief academic officer is responsible for distance education. A dean of distance learning shoulders this responsibility at the remaining institutions. The interviews focused on the following areas: program overview, institutional support, planning for online courses, and digital divide concerns. The following sections summarize selected responses from these interviews.

Program Overview.   In his study of distance education, Cejda (2007) explained that rural community colleges may be using technology to field only a small segment of their available courses rather than complete degree or certificate programs. Responses from each DLA generally supported this statement. One institution offered all of its academic transfer (AT) courses online, but career and technical education (CTE) courses available in an online format were not offered in a classroom setting. Another institution offered all but 5 percent of its AT courses online. This college also offered approximately 50 to 60 percent of its CTE courses online and was planning its first online degree program.

The other institutions offered fewer online AT and CTE courses. Percentages of AT courses ranged from approximately 14 to 60 percent (mean = 34.75 percent), with CTE offerings ranging from approximately 13 to 90 percent (mean = 40.75 percent). One institution currently offers a pair of online CTE degrees, while another offers several online AT and CTE degrees and certificate programs. Two colleges were restricted from offering entire programs online because of certain institutional commitments.

When asked about the potential to expand online course offerings, the DLAs all responded with the same limiting factor: qualified faculty members, both full time and adjunct. One individual indicated that the institution had recently reduced its number of online sections and raised the enrollment levels for each of these courses to compensate for the shortage of instructors. Two DLAs also voiced another limiting factor: bandwidth saturation. Both individuals explained that although their respective colleges had recently increased system bandwidth, constant updates to and expansion of the online instructional program had again pushed each network into approaching its maximum capacity.

Institutional Support. To better understand the importance these colleges attach to their online instructional program, the DLAs listed the number of personnel assigned to the distance education function and described each individual's specific responsibilities. One DLA has two full-time subordinates who provide basic services and expertise to support the development and delivery of online courses. Instructional technology (IT) support is outsourced at this institution. Another DLA has three full-time subordinates assigned, two of whom are involved in technology training and instruction. The third person oversees the technology equipment in the distance learning classrooms. At this college, IT also reports to the DLA.

A third DLA has a pair of subordinates directly responsible for ensuring the quality of online courses. They jointly manage the program, and one of them also serves as an e-learning specialist. Distance education and IT are in separate units at this college. Another DLA reported having eight full-time subordinates. In addition to four IT specialists, distance education at this college includes a full-time secretary, a coordinator to handle dual-credit and consortium activities, an instructional support person for course management system issues, and a test coordinator. The fifth DLA has no subordinates assigned to support distance education. In addition, this DLA is responsible for all IT issues at the college. Five personnel support this IT function. The remaining DLA has one additional person who is primarily involved with the dual-credit program. This DLA stated that IT is not part of distance education, and most maintenance functions are contracted to an outside organization.

At all six colleges, the distance education budget is directly linked to the institutional budget. Most of this budgeting involves instructor costs and expenses for technology upgrades and maintenance. While discussing the budgeting process, the DLAs mentioned the use of various fees to offset some of the costs associated with distance education. Only one of the six rural community colleges does not currently charge a technology fee or some other type of distance education or online course fee. Other interviewees indicated that although their institutions are sensitive to the rising costs of higher education, they nevertheless charge one or two types of fees: a technology fee per semester (ranging from five dollars to thirty dollars) or a distance learning/online course fee (ranging from ten dollars to twenty-five dollars per credit hour or twenty-five dollars to fifty dollars per course), or both. These fees revert back to the general fund at each college.

Planning for Online Courses.   All six DLAs indicated that their institutional master plan includes an annex devoted to distance education. Two DLAs said that the institutional master plan spans a five-year time frame. All of the remaining master plans cover one year. Each DLA related very different perspectives regarding planning for developing and sustaining online instructional programs. One individual characterized the institutional planning process as being poor and conducted in a haphazard manner, with personnel reacting to situations as they arise. Another DLA indicated that a distance learning committee supports the online instructional program of the college, but this committee does not participate in planning activities. Instead the DLA shoulders all of this responsibility. At this college, planning is limited primarily to ensuring that current online courses are scheduled to meet student demand, qualified instructors are available, and equipment remains functional. The other four rural community colleges use an advisory committee to assist developing and sustaining online courses. These committees, comprising faculty members, instructional administrators, and distance education staff, review all policies and procedures related to online instruction and use enrollment trends and student feedback to schedule future courses.

In conjunction with the planning process for online instructional programs, each DLA was asked to describe the procedures for developing and assessing online courses. At one institution, a small group of veteran online instructors and other individuals knowledgeable about distance education issues oversees the creation of the courses, and a lead faculty member serves as a mentor to help instructors construct courses. A DLA at another institution indicated that instructor desire typically fuels the creation of a new course. Since many faculty members at this institution have experience with online courses, instructors design a new class and present it for review and approval. Group discussions with faculty members, division chairs, and program directors serve as the catalyst for the development of online courses at another institution. A different DLA indicated that after establishing the need for a specific course, the institution's biggest challenges were to select the right instructor and work with him or her to decide how best to deliver the course.

Despite differences in how they plan for developing online courses, all six DLAs indicated that student feedback plays a crucial role in the assessment of these classes. To garner feedback about its online courses, one rural community college uses a midterm assessment process, augmented by informal comments. This assessment asks for feedback in five areas: instructor proficiency with the online platform and the student's level of performance in the class, overall computer skills, online course skills, and satisfaction with the class. Other institutions use an online course survey form to collect feedback regarding course content and instructor proficiency. One DLA also indicated that his institution conducts student forums to exchange ideas about online course quality and offerings.

Regardless of the level of planning for developing and assessing these courses, much of the success in fielding quality instructional programs hinges on faculty availability. One DLA, when asked about the persistent difficulties in finding full- and part-time instructors to teach online courses, joked that the task often comes down to two criteria: academic credentials and a warm pulse. Another DLA indicated that even when adjunct instructors are available, rarely does the institution assign them to an online course. Instead, these adjuncts are assigned to a face-to-face course, something that theoretically makes a full-time instructor available for online work.

Training for online instruction varied greatly among the institutions. At one college, the DLA serves as the trainer and certifying official for full- and part-time online instructors. The institution conducts a week-long training session for online course certification. Training for instructors with extensive experience is typically waived. At another institution, prospective online instructors must complete two semesters of in-house training at least one year before the course is taught. This training focuses on both pedagogical concerns and course construction issues. Instructors who demonstrate an extensive background in online instruction can be exempted from this training. The rapid increase in demand for online courses, without sufficient instructor training, caused quality issues at another institution. Now all online instructors must successfully complete a series of training modules that emphasize standardization and quality.

A different DLA stated that the institution recently reassessed its training and certification efforts after receiving adverse feedback about various online courses. The institution has decided to explore different options for increasing future training and certification requirements. At another institution, past problems in the content and delivery of all distance education courses have led to greater oversight of those who teach online courses and additional mentoring of faculty instruction. Training for online instruction is now scheduled on a regular basis, and faculty members are given adequate planning time to construct their courses.

All DLAs indicated that their respective institutions provide some type of monetary incentive linked to online course development or delivery. At one of the colleges, faculty complete the week-long training and certification process for online instruction, and after they successfully deliver a course, the college provides each faculty member with a stipend of five hundred dollars. A subsequent delivery of the course is rewarded with a per capita stipend. Another DLA indicated that the institution initially paid healthy development and delivery stipends when online courses were first made available. Due in part to technology advancements, instructors at this college are no longer paid a creation stipend. This institution currently pays a small per capita stipend that is capped at two classes per semester, with a maximum of fifty students per section. Instead of paying per capita stipends, the remaining four institutions pay instructors varying amounts, ranging from three hundred to a thousand dollars, for online course development and/or delivery.

Besides faculty issues, bandwidth concerns continue to serve as a major planning problem for online courses. One DLA reiterated that from a course development standpoint, instructors must keep things simple because of bandwidth, since many online students still rely on dial-up service. A different DLA echoed this same concern, but also indicated that the majority of the college's online students reside outside the local county, where Internet service is better. At another institution, the burgeoning online population at a branch campus has forced institutional planners to work on tripling the available bandwidth, an effort that costs both time and money. Planning is currently underway to look at possible corrective actions.

Discussion

Each of the rural community colleges showcased in this chapter has developed a variety of online courses to improve the educational reach of the institution and build student enrollments. While understandably proud of how their respective online instructional programs routinely meet the monetary, personnel, and digital divide challenges these colleges face, the DLAs also collectively exposed a major flaw: the absence of a long-range institution-wide planning process to inform resource allocation and chart future growth and sustainability. To varying degrees, planning for the development and delivery of online courses at these institutions continues to have a short-term focus at best and a reactive approach at worst. The continued growth of and demand for online courses require colleges to commit to in-depth planning, especially in the face of dwindling resources. If a college intends to harness the full range of capabilities offered by online technology, the entire institution needs to make a commitment to planning and resource allocation. Minimally, institutions need to determine what resources, including personnel, are essential to the maintenance of the online course delivery commitment; how many courses can reasonably be offered online, given available resources; which courses are best suited for online delivery; and what limits, if any, should be placed on the expansion of online offerings. Ideally, institutions need to make a concerted commitment to the inclusion of online course planning to all strategic planning procedures.

New Directions for Community Colleges • DOI: 10.1002/cc

References

Allen, E., and Seaman, J. *Making the Grade: Online Education in the United States, 2006.* Newburyport, Mass.: Sloan Consortium, 2006.

Baltzer, J. A. *The Learning Action Plan: A New Approach to Information Technology Planning in Community Colleges.* Boulder, Colo.: CAUSE, 1994.

Bathe, J. "Love It, Hate It, or Don't Care: Views on Online Learning." League for Innovation in the Community College: Conference on Information Technology, 2001. (ED 463 805) Retrieved April 21, 2010 from http://www.eric.ed.gov/ERICWebPortal/custom/portlets/recordDetails/detailmini.jsp?_nfpb=true&_&ERICExtSearch_Search Value_0=ED463805&ERICExtSearch_SearchType_0=no&accno=ED463805

Cejda, B. D. "Connecting to the Larger World: Distance Education in Rural Community Colleges." In P. L. Eddy and J. P. Murray (eds.), *Rural Community Colleges: Teaching, Learning, and Leading in the Heartland.* New Directions for Community Colleges, no. 137. San Francisco: Jossey-Bass, 2007.

Downey, S. "Strategic Planning of Online Instructional Programs: Practitioner's Perspective." *International Journal of Educational Technology,* 2001, *2*(2). Retrieved Apr. 13, 2009, from http://www.ed.uiuc.edu/ijet/v2n2/downey/index.html.

League for Innovation in the Community College. *Planning Guide for Instructional Computing Resources.* Mission Viejo, Calif.: Author, 1989.

Mupinga, D. M., and Maughan, G. R. "Web-Based Instruction and Community College Faculty Workload." *College Teaching,* 2008, *56*(1), 17-21.

Murray, J. P. "Recruiting and Retaining Rural Community College Faculty." In P. L. Eddy and J. P. Murray (eds.), *Rural Community Colleges: Teaching, Learning, and Leading in the Heartland.* New Directions for Community Colleges, no. 137. San Francisco: Jossey-Bass, 2007.

Page, G. A., and Hill, M. "Information, Communication, and Educational Technologies in Rural Alaska." In J. A. Ritchey (ed.), *Adult Education in the Rural Context: People, Place, and Change.* New Directions for Adult and Continuing Education, no. 117. San Francisco: Jossey-Bass, 2008.

Pisel, K. P. "A Strategic Planning Process Model for Distance Education." *Online Journal of Distance Learning Administration,* 2008, *11*(2). Retrieved May 7, 2009, from http://www.westga.edu/~distance/ojdla/summer112/pisel112.html.

Sink, D. W., and Jackson, K. L. "Bridging the Digital Divide: A Collaborative Approach." *Community College Journal,* 2000, *71*(2), 38-41.

Travis, J. "Ocotillo: A Management Model of Technology Infusion/Implementation." *Vision,* 1992, *4*(2), 12-15.

Travis, J. E., and Price, K. F. "Instructional Culture and Distance Learning." *Journal of Faculty Development,* 2005, *20*, 99-103.

JAY LEIST is assistant professor of higher education at Texas A&M University–Commerce in Commerce, Texas.

JON TRAVIS is professor of higher education and director of the higher education program at Texas A&M University–Commerce in Commerce, Texas.

3

Development of online learning courses and programs in colleges and universities has changed the teaching and learning environment and many institutional processes and systems over the past decade. This chapter describes the changes, challenges, and rewards of developing an online learning program by a small rural community college in central Michigan.

Administrative Challenges and Rewards of Online Learning in a Rural Community College: Reflections of a Distance Learning Administrator

Gwladys A. Austin

Mid Michigan Community College (MMCC) is a small, rural institution with three campuses in central Michigan. The college was founded in 1965 and now offers over sixty degree programs. They include transfer programs designed for students intending to go on to baccalaureate degree-granting institutions and career programs that provide students with the necessary skills and related knowledge to qualify for skilled, technical, and semiprofessional positions in business, industry, and the allied health fields. The college has a statewide reputation for its first-rate nursing and radiographic technology programs.

During the 1990s it became evident that technology was changing instructional delivery and many student and academic support services in a major way. These changes, coupled with increasing interest in and demand for more flexible scheduling for courses and programs, paved the way for colleges and universities to develop online (Web-based) courses. Within a few years, online courses became dominant as the preferred distance delivery method driven by student demand. In fact, community colleges are outpacing other higher education institutions in the development and growth of distance learning programs. The Sloan Consortium reported that over 3.9 million students took at least one online course during the fall

New Directions for Community Colleges, no. 150, Summer 2010 © 2010 Wiley Periodicals, Inc.
Published online in Wiley InterScience (www.interscience.wiley.com) • DOI: 10.1002/cc.402

2007 term, a 12 percent increase over the number reported the previous year (Allen and Seaman, 2008). The report also shows that the majority of these courses continue to be taken at two-year colleges.

Many of these factors drove the decision to fund the development of an online learning program at MMCC. In 1993 the college purchased a permanent site for offering classes in Mt. Pleasant, Michigan, twenty-eight miles south of the college's main campus in Harrison, Michigan. MMCC's main campus is located in a rural area with a population of about twenty-one hundred people and has limited broadband Internet services. The new site in Mt. Pleasant is located in a town of twenty-six thousand people that has greater resources due to the proximity of the state's fourth largest public university, Central Michigan University. Student demand for online classes and services was much stronger at that time at the secondary site than in our rural community. Other key factors contributing to MMCC's decision to offer online courses included improving student access and providing a long-term revenue stream.

Nationally the primary forces of economics and access are driving the explosive growth of distance education, which is rapidly transforming postsecondary education. Distance learning is becoming a popular choice for continuing professional education, midcareer degree programs, and lifelong learning of all kinds (Moller, Foshay, and Huett, 2008). Currently MMCC has a robust online learning program that has contributed to transformative change in the way the college offers courses, programs, student, and academic support services; use of the college's Web site; and college-wide communication. Online enrollment hovers at 14 to 15 percent of the total enrollment, with future plans to increase enrollment to meet student demand.

Considering the trends of increasing transportation and university tuition costs, growth in online learning will likely continue. According to the Sloan Consortium report (2007), "Future growth in online enrollments will no doubt flow from those institutions that are currently the most engaged; they enroll the most online learning students and have the highest expectations for growth" (p. 2). Accordingly, more of the established two-year colleges offering online courses may begin to develop completing online programs. My contention is that the implementation and rapid growth of MMCC's distance learning program has affected multiple areas of the organization and created areas of transformational change. An overview of these changes and how they influenced faculty, academic and student support services, and other divisions within the colleges will be explored.

Development and Implementation

A past president of MMCC, Ronald Verch, understood that in order for the college to meet student demand and grow as an institution, it must locate the funds to promote the development of online courses and programs.

Although this decision caused some professional consternation and accreditation challenges, it also promised new and welcomed revenue streams to support operations and future growth. In addition, offering flexible delivery options might allow more students the opportunity to further their educational goals and prepare them for the rapidly changing workplace.

In the fall of 1998, a small group of faculty and the new distance education (DE) department staff worked together to select a learning management system, develop initial courses, and set in place trial practices and procedures. As faculty developed the first online courses (nine sections in total) to be offered in the winter 1999 semester, the DE staff began working with instructional administrators and student services personnel to schedule the new online courses and develop criteria for advising students who were interested in taking these courses.

Many practices and procedures needed adjustments to accommodate on-site and online services and academic support for students. For example, frontline enrollment personnel had to provide additional information about how students logged on to their orientation and courses. The DE staff created new methods of regularly communicating with faculty and students to assist with other emerging issues once classes were live. It became readily apparent that a system was needed for assessing student readiness for online courses and that training was necessary for advisors who placed students in online courses. Faculty and instructional administrators worked with the DE staff to develop early assessment methods of online courses and determine what type of training was needed for course development and online teaching.

A majority of the early adopters were highly motivated to build a successful online program and were flexible about piloting development and teaching before negotiating academic ownership and pay issues. This collaborative spirit and interest helped address early challenges and provided the necessary components of the fledgling courses. After the first trial semester, a lead faculty member worked with DE staff to develop recommendations for contract language, which was adopted during the spring and summer 2000 negotiations with the faculty group. This cooperative relationship greatly contributed to the quality and early growth of the online program. Over time, more faculty members began developing and teaching online courses and even began using some online communication tools in on-site courses. Both full-time and adjunct faculty members participated in training and in the development and teaching of online courses.

Support for online learning from the college library and Academic Support Center personnel was also strong, and both departments worked with faculty and DE staff to develop systems to support online learners. Some services were easier to provide, such as links to online databases through the library, while others, such as a system for online tutoring and academic advising, took years to fully develop. Individuals from both departments attended the Educational Teleconsortium of Michigan and

Michigan Community College Virtual Learning Collaborative (MCCVLC) meetings and trainings to gather information and to learn how to best offer online services.

The same collaborative spirit did not initially exist with all college employees, however. Some frontline personnel resisted providing students with additional information they needed when considering an online course or program. Several of the academic advisors were suspicious of the online format and told students, particularly first-year students, to steer clear of online courses. In many areas, there was strong resistance to the necessary changes to everyday practices that an online learning program required. As these issues emerged, the DE staff realized that more education was needed concerning the online format, along with more assessment of student success in online classes. They began attending and presenting information at student services meetings and assisting with registration. They also included student services personnel in training sessions, such as the online orientation course for students. As the understanding of online services and procedures grew, resistance lessened, and better-informed registration and advising processes were developed.

Challenges and Opportunities

One significant challenge the college faces is staffing because the development of quality online courses requires experienced instructional designers and greater assistance with video and multimedia components. MMCC recently completed an external audit of all technology, including infrastructure, media, and online learning support, which will help us properly place staff members to provide better service. The importance of a full-time online instructional designer is becoming more and more evident and will provide the faculty with additional individual and small group support. In addition, the college is again entering into contract negotiations with the faculty group and will grapple with many of the other issues that linger, such as online class size.

Other issues facing the college are debates about the training and credentials of online faculty and student authentication. Instructional administrators and DE staff believe that online faculty members need to regularly update their skills, including the use of learning management system tools, to provide a rich educational experience for students. Thus, conversations regarding training and credentials are ongoing among various college units. The issue of authentication of students in an online environment is of interest not only to college employees but also for the Higher Learning Commission and the federal government. The federal government in particular is pushing those who provide online courses and programs to develop methods of identifying who is logging into online courses and being able to authenticate that the student enrolled is actually doing the course work. As in the past, the government is also concerned with actual seat time and wants colleges and universities to have systems that track the amount of time students spend reading and completing online course work.

Historically community colleges in Michigan have been regional institutions, focused on direct student and community needs. For a rural college, this focus can limit programmatic choices and cultural diversity for students and the college community. Finding ways to promote and develop options for students and provide a rich educational experience is important to the vitality of MMCC. Recent research focuses on an inclusive approach to the online learning environment and how it provides additional diversity in curricula. With careful planning and design that includes a focus on providing community college students with global concepts and perspectives, online courses and programs can help bring the outside world to rural students. The online communication tools in learning management systems provide easy access to resources and images that can strongly promote multicultural issues, thus broadening students' worldviews:

> The impact of ever-increasing numbers of online courses on the demographic composition of classes has meant that the notions of diversity, multiculturality and globalization are now key aspects of curriculum planning. For example, how do we integrate and address this multicultural dimension in a distance education course aimed at students who live in diverse cultural environments? [Germain-Rutherford and Kerr, 2008, p. 64].

Developing courses that provide a global perspective and are multicultural can be especially important to rural community colleges and their students who may not have other chances to learn about or experience other cultures. Increasingly, the Higher Learning Commission (2003) and other accrediting bodies are focusing on diversity and the importance of providing an educational environment that is inclusive of many cultures.

Other important areas of diversity and inclusion that need to be considered when developing programming include nontraditional, commuter, working, and disabled students. In addition, research has examined the needs of women as a diverse group of learners. Terry Muller studied the persistence of women in online programs and concluded that these programs held a great deal of promise for women learners: "Career, family, and community obligations often do not allow adult women to enroll in conventional college programs. Convenient access to distance-learning courses, however, can provide them with education and/or training. Online courses promise learners access, flexibility, and convenience" (2008, para. 1).

Ensuring student success through developing systems that provide regular assessment and related improvements remains a high priority for MMCC. The college regularly tracks and compares online student success and retention to on-site students. A current issue under negotiation centers on online student evaluation of full-time online faculty members. A system is being developed and spearheaded by a new adjunct faculty coordinator to conduct student evaluations every semester for adjunct faculty who teach online courses. Some of the full-time faculty members do not support the same system being applied in their online classes because the evaluation practice would differ from their on-site student evaluations. Another area of great interest to the faculty and administration is tracking the growth and development of hybrid courses. Equal quality standards applied to online, hybrid, and on-site courses would enhance development and fit with best practices, but they are not currently an area of agreement.

It is also vital that MMCC provide robust academic and student services to all students, both on-site and online. These services are improving, but additional resources are needed to make them available at all times. Some academic support services for online students are provided collaboratively through the MCCVLC, which helps small community colleges like MMCC leverage resources. The college's IT department is also investigating ways to provide redundancy and backup for servers, firewalls, and Internet pipelines and services to ensure connectivity for online students and faculty.

Improvements and Benefits

Early online course development focused on particular courses that were mainly from the arts and sciences curricula. As our experience grew and the expertise of the faculty and distance learning staff increased, other academic areas were considered for development. According to the National Research Center for Career and Technical Education (Johnson & Benson, 2003), the development of distance learning courses or programs had not previously focused on vocational or technical education. Therefore the authors of the report indicated that due to the Internet, advances in computers, and multimedia resources, community colleges have expanded their distance learning programs to include career and technical courses. Indeed increased interest in occupational course development has been the case at MMCC, where in the past two years, the didactic courses for the level one and two nursing program have been successfully developed and placed online. The podcasting of lectures for these courses has been so popular that on-site students soon demanded access to the podcasts as well. Other health-related programs, including the physical therapy assistant and medical terminology programs, are now asking for increased online components or development of online and hybrid courses.

Over time, increasing emphasis has been placed on course quality, which has improved student retention and success in online courses. For the past few years, the success rates and retention of online students have been the same as for on-site students. To reach these outcomes, the DE staff has worked with faculty and deans in either significantly revising online courses or at times pulling particular online courses out of regular on-site offerings. For example, one particular course, speech, is no longer offered online because the local university would not accept transfer of an online speech course.

MMCC also collaborates with other community colleges in the development of shared programs that offer either on-site or online course work with our college and online or on-site completion course work at the partner college. These shared programs allow students to select programs that MMCC would not be able to offer alone. The travel to the other colleges is reduced for students with the combination of some course work at MMCC and some online courses from the partner college.

Institutional Change

Implementing any change in an established institution takes leadership and commitment. Developing and implementing a quality online learning program involves substantial organizational change. Van Dusen (1997) stated that the primary constraint in establishing an online program is neither technical nor pedagogical but organizational and social in nature. Overcoming organizational obstacles requires leadership and responsibility for promoting the many changes required for implementing a quality program. Over time, organizational change has increased as technology has pushed change throughout the institution. Evolving technology has modified the way people do their jobs at the college, along with the way we communicate internally and externally. Keeping up-to-date on the regularly changing technical requirements for state, federal, and accreditation reports is daunting.

As the online program at MMCC became institutionalized, many processes were transformed. A transformational change must take place in order for online education to be a successful and integral part of a college (Garza Mitchell, 2008). For MMCC, this transformation created many rewards for students and faculty, including a delivery system that allowed all students to have a voice in the virtual classroom and a multimedia online environment that supports student learning in new ways. Faculty and DE staff researched best practices, and as these strategies were incorporated into the online classes, it soon became apparent that these best practices would also be useful for on-site classrooms.

Another important benefit of developing online classes was increased access for the local high school dual-enrolled students, thus helping to enrich curriculum in the rural K-12 school districts. The flexibility of scheduling course work was a direct benefit for all online learners. Dillon and Cintron (1997) considered the promise of distance education to be increased access. Those who promote distance technologies cite their potential to reach disabled, homebound, isolated, and economically and educationally disadvantaged students. In a poor, rural area with limited mass transit and limited options for K-12 curriculum, online options take on increased importance to the community.

In addition, with the ongoing loss of population in Michigan, a quality, robust online program becomes a viable method to increase enrollments outside the state. Other states are also increasingly looking at educational options due to declining populations or birth rates. A 2009 report commissioned by the Ohio Board of Regents of the University System discussed the declining youth population and the resulting narrowing of the traditional pipeline of high school students. The report concluded that the state must rely on attracting into the educational system older adults who are interested in obtaining a college degree. To do this, the report notes that "Ohio must increase its use of technology, aggressively grow E-Learning, and promote greater student interface with technology as strategies to increase success and effect greater efficiencies in administrative and academic functions" (p. 12).

Developing online learning programs appears to be increasingly a strong component in strategic planning for institutions of higher education, particularly in certain academic areas that lend themselves to online or hybrid development. According to Minsun Shin and Yoon-Joo Lee (2009), "Sixty-seven percent of colleges and universities agree that online education is the single significant development and logical long-term strategy for the field of teacher preparation, offering flexibility and convenience by providing learning opportunities to anyone, at anytime, and anywhere."

Conclusions and Lessons Learned

The impact of creating and implementing an online education program at MMCC was substantial and in many ways transformational. Almost all areas of the college experienced changes to their processes due to the development of our online program. The first lesson learned was that regular and intentional communication and targeted training play a significant role in gaining employee acceptance for these changes. This communication must include all college departments, students, transfer institutions, local businesses, and community members to be highly effective. Training also must be offered and promoted to those who teach, provide services, or are involved in the enrollment management process at the college or university. Without training and a basic understanding of the delivery option, individuals and departments may well work against the implementation.

Another lesson learned is that community colleges can extend their regional outreach with online offerings. In particular, the importance of maintaining a robust online program in a Michigan community college becomes more and more evident as the state struggles with economic decline and population migration to other states. MMCC currently offers an average of fifty courses with ninety sections and approximately nineteen hundred unduplicated students per major (fall and winter) semester. This contributes 14 to 15 percent of the college's total credit hours each year.

NEW DIRECTIONS FOR COMMUNITY COLLEGES • DOI: 10.1002/cc

Increasing this portion of the total enrollment is strategic for MMCC's future viability.

Fortunately, increasing student online enrollment does not include some of the costs necessary for on-site instruction. Michigan and other states across the country are trying to contain costs and are backing away from the responsibility of funding a significant percentage of operational, deferred maintenance, and construction costs for new buildings. However, most staffing costs are a factor because it is vital to hire and retain quality faculty and DE professionals who will develop online courses and programs that support all student learning styles and strengthen the teaching and learning environment.

An important lesson learned is that developing and offering online classes promoted teaching and learning changes in the online and on-site classrooms. Faculty discussion now addresses topics such as online student learning and how multimedia tools can enrich instruction in both online and on-site classes. This dialogue has created new instructional strategies for all delivery formats. Faculty members share ideas during meetings and training sessions, often leading to changes and improvements in teaching techniques. The use of multimedia tools in online classes also has increased faculty demand for multimedia equipment in all classrooms. The college is now very close to its goal of providing standardized multimedia equipment carts in every classroom due to the efforts of the library and media services director. This improvement makes training much easier and increases faculty use of multimedia equipment.

Offering multiple educational delivery options fits closely with goals from MMCC strategic planning and allows better access for students. It also provides a method of extending outreach to out-of-state students as competition increases for a declining number of students in Michigan. Finally, our local K-12 schools are hardest hit by state cutbacks and have been forced to make serious budget cuts that include teachers and curricular offerings. Fortunately, providing high-quality and diverse online classes for dual-enrolled high school students can supplement their educational options.

Suggestions for Practice

The most important suggestion for institutions considering the development and implementation of online courses and programs is to bring all stakeholders into the planning process. Without the buy-in of faculty and the related academic and student support departments, the implementation will be much more difficult, and it may not be successful. Schools that have attempted to build an online program that is totally separate from the academic divisions appear to have ongoing competition between the academic and online programs.

My other suggestion is to promote online delivery quality by encouraging faculty to engage in peer review of their online courses and regularly

NEW DIRECTIONS FOR COMMUNITY COLLEGES • DOI: 10.1002/cc

involve students when developing new courses or programs. We received a great deal of important feedback from students when we conducted regular focus meetings with them while we were developing the online didactic courses for our nursing program. This feedback saved us time, avoided mistakes, and also helped develop some best practices in blending online and on-site courses.

References

Allen, I. E., and Seaman, J. *Staying the Course: Online Education in the United States, 2008*. Needham, Mass.: Sloan Consortium, 2008.

Dillon, C. L., and Cintron, R. "Distance Education and the Community College: From Convention to Vision." In C. L. Dillon and R. Cintron (eds.), *Building a Working Policy for Distance Education*. New Directions for Community Colleges, no. 99. San Francisco: Jossey-Bass, 1997.

Garza Mitchell, R. L. "Online Education in the Community College: Individual, Group, and Organizational Perceptions of Change." Unpublished doctoral dissertation, Central Michigan University, 2008.

Germain-Rutherford, A., and Kerr, B. "An Inclusive Approach to Online Learning Environments: Models and Resources." *Turkish Online Journal of Distance Education*, 2008, 9(2), 64-85.

Higher Learning Commission. "Institutional Accreditation: An Overview." 2003. Retrieved June 13, 2009, from http://www.ncahlc.org/index.php?option=com_docman&task=cat_view&Itemid=229&gid=63.

Johnson, S. D., and Benson, A. D. "Distance Learning in Postsecondary Career and Technical Education." 2003. Retrieved June 6, 2009, from www.nccte.org/publications/infosynthesis/r&dreport/Distance_Learning_Post_CTE.pdf

Minsun, S., and Yoon-Joo, L. "Changing the Landscape of Teacher Education via Online Teaching and Learning." *Technologies,84*(1) 2009. Retrieved June, 6, 2009, from http://www.acteonline.org.

Moller, L., Foshay, W. R., and Huett, J. "The Evolution of Distance Education: Implications for Instructional Design on the Potential of the Web." *Tech Trends*, 2008, 52(4), 66-71.

Muller, T. "Persistence of Women in Online Degree-Completion Programs." *International Review of Research in Open and Distance Learning*, 2008, 9(2), 1492-3831.

Ohio Board of Regents. *Second Report on the Condition of Higher Education in Ohio: Meeting the State's Future Needs through a Competitive Higher Education Facility and Technology Infrastructure*. Retrieved June 6, 2009, from http://uso.edu/downloads/reports/.

Van Dusen, G. C. *The Virtual Campus: Technology and Reform in Higher Education*. Washington, D.C.: George Washington University, 1997.

GWLADYS A. AUSTIN is vice president of technology and institutional services at Mid Michigan Community College, Harrison, Michigan.

NEW DIRECTIONS FOR COMMUNITY COLLEGES • DOI: 10.1002/cc

4

The rate of expansion of online classes at community colleges has required hiring and training faculty for the online class offerings. The demand is being met in large part by adjunct faculty, who, as with face-to-face classes, continue to represent a large portion of the community college online faculty.

The Trials and Accomplishments of an Online Adjunct Faculty Member

Jeffrey Hoyle

In January 2004 I decided to pursue a doctorate. Due to the time commitments of my current position as a faculty member at a four-year college and my family, I determined that an online program from an accredited institution was the only feasible way to pursue a Ph.D. at that time.

The online process was a change from the traditional classroom that I was familiar with. Although I was aware of the classroom management system (CMS) used on my campus, which had I incorporated into my classes, the orientation to my online degree program introduced me to the process of learning online, and I came to view the online environment as a legitimate form of learning.

About a year after I began my online program, I received an e-mail about an online teaching opportunity. This came about as a result of a meeting I attended where the interim dean of City Colleges of Chicago (CCC) discussed the growing demand for quality instructors to teach online for the rapidly expanding online segment of its Center for Distance Learning (CDL). Based on my positive learning experience, I took the opportunity to get in on the ground floor of a new and growing form of teaching and applied for an adjunct teaching position with CCC for the summer of 2006. I quickly found myself in a new environment of teaching, collaboration, and assessment. This chapter documents my journey as an adjunct online instructor at City Colleges of Chicago Center for Distance Learning.

NEW DIRECTIONS FOR COMMUNITY COLLEGES, no. 150, Summer 2010 © 2010 Wiley Periodicals, Inc.
Published online in Wiley InterScience (www.interscience.wiley.com) • DOI: 10.1002/cc.403

Training for the Virtual Classroom

Being an online student in a doctoral program was a tremendous help in providing a student's perspective of the online experience. I used this perspective when it came to designing my own online course to ensure I communicated clearly and often. I could also appreciate the fact that technology did not always work as planned, which prepared me to address this issue and alert students before they encountered technical glitches. A favorite saying I use in class is, "Technology is great . . . when it works." This serves as a good icebreaker for students, especially those taking their first online course.

The training that was required for new CCC online instructors and facilitators included a mandatory course, Online Learning: An Overview, which was offered by the Illinois Online Network (ION). Other ION classes required within the first two years of online teaching for CCC were Encouraging Communication in Online Courses and Instructional Design for Online Course Development. The ION master online teacher certificate (MOT) was not required to teach at CCC, but it was encouraged.

I went on to complete the MOT in 2008, and the program has provided an excellent knowledge base for teaching online classes. The ION sessions required for the MOT usually had several CCC adjunct faculty enrolled, and fostered collaboration on projects for these classes as well as sharing CCC and CDL experiences and ideas. These classes were good not only for the content but also because I had to struggle with how to use technology in my own virtual classroom experiences. This encounter with technology caused me to have empathy for students and not be too quick to assume that students who asked for an extension or help on an assignment or project were trying to abuse the system.

The Challenge of Physical Distance

I found it challenging from an instructor's perspective to function in the online environment and wondered what students looked and sounded like and what their body language might convey. This new venue also came with the challenges of learning how to conduct online classes and understanding my role as a teacher. CCC used the term *facilitator* in many of the training sessions. A facilitator was associated with a more hands-off constructivist approach to allow students to figure out for themselves how to assimilate and apply the material presented (Meyer, 2002).

I developed a teaching philosophy that focused on the problem-solving process, not just on getting the correct answer. This required me to resist intervening and correcting what I might perceive as a wrong or incorrect approach. I needed to let students make mistakes in order to learn and encouraged them to discuss the reasoning behind solutions rather than focusing only on the answers, which differed from my face-to-face teaching

NEW DIRECTIONS FOR COMMUNITY COLLEGES • DOI: 10.1002/cc

techniques at the time. My own engagement in this online teaching and learning environment helped me better understand how to facilitate learning, and I began to understand why *facilitator* was not only a better word for *teacher, professor,* or *instructor* but a better approach to both the face-to-face and online classrooms. Certain issues such as distractions, shyness, and status that might cause stereotyping in the traditional classroom were removed, or at least had a lower profile, in the virtual setting.

Through trial and error, combined with training in how to engage online students, I learned how to write thoughtful questions for my discussion boards. As I asked better questions, I found that the answers posted by students began to improve from a critical thinking perspective. This led to the sharing of different opinions and respectful disagreement, which I had not experienced in the face-to-face classroom, and it became the norm in my online classes. Once I figured out how to ask better questions, offer limited input, and help guide discussions, engaged dialogue continued to grow.

In addition to learning how to conduct a class in the virtual classroom, I also had to learn how to deal with administrative issues virtually. I had had online ethics training sessions, required by both CCC and the State of Illinois, and had to submit payroll, human resource, and other forms either online or by fax or regular mail. I even had to give permission for certain staff members to execute my employment contracts because I was not on campus and CCC does not accept faxed or process contracts electronically. Although the staff were usually very helpful, at times it was challenging to find the right person to speak to about a specific topic as many staff members wear multiple hats due to turnover, promotions, and growth at CCC.

Each semester, about two weeks before classes start, there are mandatory online synchronous faculty orientation sessions with the dean of the CDL, instructional designers, student services, and technical support staff. The sessions cover such topics as the academic calendar, how to determine if students are active participants, what to do if they are not, how to communicate with students and administrators, where to find policy manuals, and to whom to address questions about policy or specific situations in class, as well as other issues that may come up in the course of a session.

After the session a recording with supporting documentation is made available for future reference. CCC will not allow anyone to teach who has not attended or listened to a recording of these sessions. There is a question-and-answer component of these meetings, as well as individual sessions with a specific instructor or designer if issues are still not clear to a specific individual. In these sessions, it was emphasized that CCC online students are very qualified, although instructors are encouraged and expected to go "the extra mile" and do some "hand holding" and advising should it be needed. Facilitators were encouraged to ask for help if they came across an issue they may not have dealt with in the past. After going through training, I found myself making many follow-up phone calls to students as to why they had not logged in to the classroom and found that most had legitimate reasons. This awakened me to another important aspect of the online classroom in the community college setting: many students had jobs, families, and other challenges to deal with in addition to making it to virtual class and keeping up with all the assignments.

Changes in the Online Environment at CCC

Increased demands for online classes at CCC came at the same time that the college was instituting an evaluation process for all online faculty, as well as accreditation visits and review. Faculty had questions as to why the administration wanted to evaluate online faculty, which included ensuring the quality of online instruction and accreditation issues. To address faculty concerns, a series of virtual and face-to-face meetings was conducted to explain the rationale for the evaluation process and how it would ensure the quality of online instruction and aid in the accreditation process. The meetings were also a good way to get feedback and help set up the trial evaluations. This approach to introducing the evaluation process was professional, and it engaged online faculty in helping to launch the trial evaluation process. The evaluation process resulted in a checklist and scoring system, as well as an agreement that each faculty member would be evaluated every two years.

The evaluation process helped me to reflect on and consider the recommendations and how they might be implemented in future courses. Shortly after my first review, I was nominated for a Best Online Course award, for which I was runner-up. Even after the evaluation process was implemented, the administration of CCC continued to seek feedback from faculty as to the usefulness of the evaluations.

Where I Stand Today

After teaching nine classes for CCC in the CDL, from summer 2006 to spring 2009, I can look back and see progress in my ability to design online courses that facilitate learning and engage students as measured by learning outcomes, student surveys, faculty evaluations, and my own surveys taken during and after courses. I have become more willing to embrace new classroom techniques, both technical and pedagogical, based on research, recommendations, and potential for improvement of my personal skills, learning outcomes, and building community in the online classroom. With the recognition of my progress also comes a realization that I must continue to strive for better ways to meet and exceed the needs of my online students. The CCC students motivate me to embrace the concept of lifelong learning— learning anytime, anywhere regardless of place and time to learn something new to better myself and others on whom I have an impact.

I am finally experiencing a sense of connection I did not feel with earlier classes, as evidenced by the fact that I am receiving requests for recommendations for students who want to transfer to four-year institutions or advance in their jobs. Students are also beginning to include me as part of their extended families by communicating about births, deaths, graduations, weddings, and other major events in their lives and the lives of their family. More than any other measure of my teaching abilities, I personally value the connection to my students' lives as a metric of success, although I am not sure how to quantify it at this time. Subjectively this connection serves to motivate me to explore new ways to connect with students personally and not just as their teacher. These relationships may be key to getting and keeping students involved in lifelong learning. As Strange and Banning (2001) observed, "The key to successful learning and, indeed, to developing students' talents, can be simply stated: 'Students learn from becoming involved'" (p. 138).

Lessons Learned and Advice for Online Adjunct Faculty

The virtual environment and the challenge of communicating and engaging students make it essential to prepare extensively, and well in advance, for the online classroom. Preparation begins with a detailed syllabus that provides specific information about when assignments are due, how they are to be submitted, how and when they will be graded, and where grades will be posted. The grading component leads to the need for detailed rubrics so that students understand the requirements (Herman, Aschbacher, and Winters, 1992). Tutorials and tools such as blogs and wikis for projects and assignments are crucial for building community and collaboration that contribute to a quality learning environment. Any use of technology needs to be evaluated for its ability to facilitate learning. Technology should not be used merely because it is new or state-of-the-art; it must be learning driven by improving the delivery and comprehension of information and must not take away from or frustrate students in their learning process (Wilson, 2003).

Do not be afraid to consider new ways to engage online students. This most likely will require training in new techniques such as podcasting, inviting a virtual guest into your online classroom using Skype, or using Second Life to illustrate a concept. If my experiences are typical, then some of these trials will not work out as planned. Do not be too quick to write off any innovative experience as a failure, though, because these trials will help you keep an open mind in considering new ways to create a collaborative learning environment in both on-site and online settings.

Online instructors have to make sure not to let any students slip through the cracks in the virtual world. The virtual classroom increases the diligence required of online facilitators to keep track of students and ensure that the goals of high retention and graduation rates at community colleges are not compromised in the online setting. Ensuring that students participate in the online class requires personal attention so that they do not get lost. As CDL online students succeed, they tell others about how the programs, faculty, and staff helped them become successful by building their self-esteem and confidence. This should result in positive word-of-mouth among CCC stakeholders and stimulate more interest in and inquiries about CCC's online programs. The future will require more dedicated CDL faculty to commit to their students and expand the horizon of online educational opportunities for students, faculty, and all stakeholders of CCC (Allen and Seaman, 2008).

I have been an adjunct instructor since 1996 at several institutions of higher education, and after completing my Ph.D., I may still be an adjunct faculty member, a title I wear with pride. Unfortunately, adjunct faculty members are sometimes viewed in a negative light, but we have the privilege of being able to place a greater emphasis on teaching, which is extremely important in the online environment (Townsend and Twombly, 2007).

Adjunct faculty at CCC account for a substantial portion of the faculty. Since adjuncts usually are paid less than full-time faculty, teach more classes, and have less attractive teaching schedules, adjunct faculty more than likely teach because they love to see students succeed. They are in it not for the money or prestige but to be part of the success of each student, one student at a time (Townsend and Twombly, 2007).

Teaching has always been my motivation, but I must confess my initial attempts at teaching were for some of the wrong reasons. As I discovered how hard it is to be a good teacher, I have come to view the challenge of the classroom, online and face-to-face, more as a gathering of individuals rather than just a gathering, and my focus on individual students has resulted in a more positive and enriching personal experience for me and my students in online and traditional classes.

References

Allen, I. E., and Seaman, J. *Staying the Course: Online Education in the United States, 2008*. Needham, Mass.: Sloan Consortium, 2008.

Herman, J. L., Aschbacher, P. R., and Winters, L. "Select or Design Assessments That Elicit Established Outcomes." 1992. Retrieved Aug. 8, 2009, from http://www.ncrel.org/sdrs/areas/issues/methods/assment/as7sele2.htm.

Meyer, K. A. *Quality in Distance Education: Focus on Online Learning*. ASHE-ERIC Higher Education Report, 29(4). San Francisco: Jossey-Bass, 2002.

Strange, C., and Banning, J. *Education by Design: Creating Campus Learning Environments That Work*. San Francisco: Jossey-Bass, 2001.

Townsend, B. K., and Twombly, S. B. *Community College Faculty: Overlooked and Undervalued*. ASHE-ERIC Higher Education Report, 32(6). San Francisco: Jossey-Bass, 2007.

Wilson, W. "Faculty Perceptions and Uses of Instructional Technology." *EDUCAUSE Quarterly*, 2003, 26(2). Retrieved July 30, 2009, from http://net.educause.edu/ir/library/pdf/eqm0329.pdf.

JEFFREY HOYLE is an adjunct online instructor at City Colleges of Chicago.

5

The professional role, tasks, and skills of online community college faculty are evolving. This chapter describes the factors that influence the skill set needed for online faculty to be successful.

Essential Tasks and Skills for Online Community College Faculty

Vernon C. Smith

A recent commentary in the *Chronicle of Higher Education* exclaimed, "I trained for it, I tried it, and I'll never do it again. While online teaching may be the wave of the future (although I desperately hope not), it is not for me" (Clift, 2009). This experienced college professor went on to lament the difficulties of communicating virtually, the design of the curriculum, the challenges and workload associated with managing the course management system, and the loss of control over familiar classroom processes. Ironically, the reasons given for not teaching online also hinted at the skills that an online faculty must master to be successful, including ways that this faculty role is transforming.

While purposely choosing not to teach online may still be possible for faculty at community colleges, this may not be an option in the future. Examine any posting for a faculty position, and notice the level of technology skills or online teaching experience that has been incorporated into the minimum job qualifications. The use of technology and the sheer volume of courses moving online in community colleges are undeniable. It is no secret that significant enrollment growth for community colleges has the greatest potential through online courses. The Instructional Technology Council (2009) survey reported an 11.3 percent increase in distance education enrollments above campus enrollments for associate's-level colleges, with an 18 percent increase from fall 2005 to fall 2006 for e-earning enrollments specifically. Allen and Seaman (2008) note that these institutions

NEW DIRECTIONS FOR COMMUNITY COLLEGES, no. 150, Summer 2010 © 2010 Wiley Periodicals, Inc.
Published online in Wiley InterScience (www.interscience.wiley.com) • DOI: 10.1002/cc.404

provide over half of all online courses to undergraduate students and are "overrepresented among the online student population compared to their share of higher education enrollments" (p. 6). It follows that if community colleges offer mostly online courses, there are community college faculty teaching those courses.

Describing an online faculty member or community college faculty member may soon be synonymous. The role of the online faculty and the knowledge and skills associated with the growth of online course enrollments are transforming the nature and characteristics of community college faculty as a profession. This transformation is highly influenced by the essential tasks needed to create and deliver an online course. To accomplish these tasks, an online community college faculty member must master new skills that incorporate new technologies and new instructional assumptions and strategies. The model for creating and delivering online courses, and the efforts by faculty members to rebundle their role, meaning to maintain control and performing all the tasks themselves influences which skills will be required to be a successful online community college faculty member. This will transform the skills, the role, and the community college faculty as a profession.

This chapter identifies the essential tasks, skills, and knowledge that online community college faculty members need to master as a profession in a dynamic time of change, including the online course production models that enhance or detract from that mastery.

Faculty as a Profession

In academia, the faculty as a profession emerged from its origins in the scholars' guild. In contrast to other craft guilds, the scholars' guild has survived in its same basic form since the Middle Ages. (Think of the robes and academic garb that we see during commencement ceremonies as an example of a Middle Age fashion show.) Community college faculty have emulated the professoriate's teaching and service roles while deemphasizing the research tasks typically associated with the university professoriate. Modern professional power rests on the ability of a profession—in this case, community college faculty—to control their membership and their workplace conditions, including the knowledge, tools, and means of production (Krause, 1996).

Changes to the professional role and its core professional power come about through a number of internal and external forces. Internal forces include the acquisition of new knowledge or skills and the internal dynamics that stratify the profession itself (Hughes, 1994). For example, the use of teaching assistants instead of tenured faculty, or part-time faculty over full-time faculty, is an example of an internal stratification that alters the nature of the profession. External forces include the introduction of new technologies, market demand, and interprofessional conflict over the pro-

NEW DIRECTIONS FOR COMMUNITY COLLEGES • DOI: 10.1002/cc

fessional domain and social movements (Abbott, 1988). New technologies, as the Internet once was, and the ability to organize work in new ways have the most profound effect on a profession and are its "central destroyer" (Abbott, 1988), meaning that technologies replace the need for human expertise embodied in a profession.

In the case of online teaching and learning, nearly all facets that challenge and shape a profession both internally and externally are present. Rhoades (1998) has noted how the professional domains of faculty are being increased, altered, or destroyed as new technologies are introduced. These new technologies and work processes may remain with faculty as they attempt to control and rebundle their role or may be championed by groups other than faculty members, for example, instructional designers.

In summary, professions complete a series of essential tasks through special skills and knowledge that they have obtained over time through affiliation with the profession. When the skills and knowledge change, or when others can obtain that knowledge and use those skills, the profession either moves to protect its knowledge or skills in its domain, or it loses control.

Essential Tasks

What are the essential tasks and the corresponding skills that an online community college faculty member must master? The answer is complex and depends on a number of factors. What is clear is that an established body of literature has described these online faculty tasks and skills in specific terms, founded in the concept of the unbundling of the faculty role.

All professions consist of bundles of tasks (Hughes, 1994). Through specialization, each of the task bundles can be unbundled and performed by substitutes: by technologies and machines or by other people who specialize in those specific tasks. In the online course context, these essential tasks needed to create and deliver an online course from the conceptualization of the course to submitting final grade rosters have gone through an identification process over the past forty years. These unbundled tasks also correspond to the literature on what skills online faculty need to master (Paulson 2002; Levin, Kater, and Wagoner, 2006; Smith and Rhoades, 2006).

Troutt (1979), who wrote before the rise of online courses, separated the teaching and assessment tasks from the teaching and advising tasks that community college faculty normally perform. Starting from Wang's (1975) notion of specialization around educational tasks or functions, Troutt described the rise of advisement centers and advisors as specialists to perform faculty tasks with the assumption that advisors would have more incentive to perform the advising tasks than faculty members would. Troutt described these roles as "a corporate rather than an individual responsibility," and he suggested that "an advisor would assume a mentor or tutor role . . . to assess what the students' needs are to guide them through their educational experience" (p. 258). Troutt identified advising, mentoring, and tutoring as separate tasks normally performed by a faculty member that could be unbundled.

Daniel (1996) described the unbundling of the faculty role at the British Open University. In a tutoring model, distance learning courses were designed and created as standardized courses. Likewise, Twigg (1996) described the unbundling of the faculty role as an essential process in the redesign of large-enrollment, technology-mediated courses. Technology substituted professional expertise in the form of course management systems; automated assessment of exercises, quizzes, and tests; and tutorials would be coupled with the substitution of lower-cost labor in order to achieve greater learning efficiencies and cost savings (Twigg, 2003). Twigg (1996) also identified four faculty tasks that could be unbundled: development of course content, delivery of instruction, mediation, and evaluation.

Jewett (2000) and Boettcher (2000) used Twigg's (1996, 2003) description of unbundled tasks in course redesign to present an economic model with unbundled tasks in order to measure productivity in distance learning courses, including online courses. Jewett collapsed the essential tasks into three functions: preparing instructional materials, presenting the materials in the classroom, and student-related tasks such as "interaction regarding course content and evaluation of homework, quizzes, examinations, projects, and papers, up to and including assignment of course grades" (p. 101–108). He further divided the student-related tasks into interaction and evaluation. Jewett commented, "This 'unbundling' of the components of faculty workload represents one of the key differences between distributed instruction (online courses) and classroom instruction when the various instructional activities . . . have usually been performed by the individual faculty member teaching classroom courses" (p. 117). In other words, the essential tasks and the skills to perform those tasks in online courses were differentiated and identifiable.

Goodyear and others (2000) reported the results of workshops involving practitioners and theorists who identified the essential competencies and the corresponding online faculty tasks: process facilitator, advisor-counselor, assessor, researcher, content facilitator, technologist, designer, and manager-administrator. In this more detailed list of essential tasks, the tasks of design and interaction became more apparent.

Paulson (2002) conceptualized five essential faculty tasks that could be unbundled but acknowledged that academic advising "could be included as a sixth activity, especially in baccalaureate institutions." She identified these faculty tasks or functions:

- Designing the course or curriculum
- Developing the course or curriculum by selecting appropriate instructional methods and course materials, or creating those course materials

- Delivering the subject matter previously selected either in person (lectures, presentations, and so forth) or through the use of various forms of media
- Mediating (also called "tutoring") the learning process, which helps students understand materials in ways tailored to their individual learning styles and levels of understanding
- Assessing individual student learning through appropriate methods and assignments designed to certify the attainment of a given level of competence.

Slaughter and Rhoades (2004) noted that the control of the intellectual property and the commodification of courses were a means of unbundling essential faculty tasks. They gave examples such as the use of specialists, part-time faculty, and low-cost faculty as ways faculty tasks were unbundled in community college online course settings. This analysis identified such specific tasks as design, delivery, evaluation, assessment, and technical and academic advising that were unbundled along lines that reduced costs, controlled intellectual property, and increased managerial control.

Levin, Kater, and Wagoner (2006), relying on Paulson's (2002) conceptualization of unbundling, indicate that community college faculty are unbundled in terms of the "loss of the professional identity as an autonomous expert" because of the use of part-time and contingent faculty, managers, and technicians to perform traditional faculty tasks. They thus recognized unbundling within the context of globalizing community colleges, in particular, with the delivery of instruction through the use of technology.

In their study of Web-based community college courses in a multi-campus urban community college district, Smith and Rhoades (2006) confirmed the essential faculty tasks that could be unbundled from the literature and identified a previously unidentified essential task: improving the online course in a systematic fashion:

- *Design.* The selection of teaching and learning pedagogies, strategies, and methods, including learning objectives, goals, and outcomes
- *Content.* The curriculum or subject matter, including the course materials and competencies needed to be presented in order to reach the objectives and expected learning outcomes
- *Development.* The creation and placement of the content in order to be viewed digitally on the Internet, usually through placement of the content into a course management system
- *Delivery.* The transmission of the developed course to students using the Internet
- *Grading.* The evaluation and feedback of student assessments (quizzes, papers, exams, portfolios, and so on)
- *Interaction.* Communication, mediation, and motivation with students

- *Improvement.* The change process to improve course effectiveness, including its documentation
- *Advising.* Answering curricular, programmatic, college, and other questions from students

Essential Skills

The essential skills that an online faculty member must master correspond to the essential tasks. The most familiar remain based on sound instruction and pedagogy: grading, interacting, advising, and content creation. Experienced faculty members know the ins and outs of grading assignments, providing feedback for student improvement, and answering questions. This is familiar ground regardless of whether the teaching is done in a classroom or online. The same may be said of content creation. Faculty members seek not only to convey the content but also inspire and cause the students to consider the subject matter in new, analytical, and critical ways.

While these tasks seem more familiar, the other essential tasks often require the faculty member to journey to new territory. Instructional design is a discipline that has made significant strides as an empirical science over the past few decades, especially with the computer and Web-based learning. New technologies cannot be overemphasized. Course management systems are now approaching their third or fourth iterations in complexity. Consider how many faculty refer to teaching their "Blackboard" or "WebCT" course instead of an "Internet" or "Web-based" course. Delivery options have also changed dramatically within the past five years. Second Life, Facebook, Twitter, smartphones, and social media or Web 2.0 means of delivery have altered the channels for delivering courses to the point that mobile learning has become a subset of online learning.

These skill sets have been confirmed in various studies. In a meta-analysis of the literature covering essential skills and knowledge for teaching online, Lee and Hirumi (2004) identified six essential skills and accompanying subskills that were consistently identified across the academic literature: in order of importance, interaction, management, organization/instructional design, technology, content knowledge, and teamwork skills. In terms of the familiar ground versus the new skill set, take note that the first two skills are familiar, while the next cluster of skills takes the faculty member into new territory. Lee and Hirumi (2004) emphasized this point when they noted, "Even though many educators urged the competency of technology in online teaching, this ranking also presents a trend that online education is driven by pedagogical concerns instead of technological concerns" (p. 536).

But even the familiar territory is changing. Interaction, management, and content knowledge no longer mean the same thing in online courses as they do in traditional courses. By definition, the application of these skills is different for online courses. Kim and Bonk (2006) reported the findings of a survey sent to over twelve thousand experienced online college professors, instructional designers, and administrators that articulated the perceived future of online teaching. Although these findings suggest that new technologies will have a significant impact on the skills online faculty must master, institutional factors and pedagogical competence are ranked as greater in importance than technological skills competence. "Monetary support" and "pedagogical competency of online instructors" precede "technical competency of online instructors" and "improvements in online technologies." Technologies were followed by "marketing" and "rigorous quality management in the accreditation process," suggesting a mix of both faculty skills and institutional support. Kim and Bonk report "that this study found that the most important [pedagogical] skills for an online instructor during the next few years will be how to moderate or facilitate learning and how to develop or plan for high-quality online courses" (p. 27). Surprisingly, breaking down the reported skills corresponds with the essential tasks required to create and deliver an online course. These skills were, in order of top ranking and percentage: course developer (66.4 percent), facilitator or moderator, (65.8 percent), subject matter expert (55.7 percent), instructor or lecturer (51.0 percent), student counselor or advisor (36.1 percent), technology trainer (30.3 percent), and program coordinator or developer (28.6 percent).

One might ask when developing a course or training in new technologies became a pedagogical skill faculty need to know. But the nature of online courses has pushed and reshaped the essential tasks and skill sets that faculty have traditionally held. This new pedagogical skill set is dominated by instructional design theories and principles that describe how to accomplish the essential online course tasks. These principles prescriptively dictate how specific online tasks should be done, especially the design tasks, and what the final product should look like. These theories and principles are the basis for new instructional assumptions and strategies for online faculty. Implicit in these instructional design principles are the skills needed to create a quality online course—the quality standard being defined by these same principles. The most advanced application of these principles, outside the many educational technology graduate programs, is Quality Matters. Quality Matters (QM) is a quality rubric based on research literature and recognized best practices for online teaching and learning. The rubric is characterized by eight quality standards divided into 40 subcategories that prescribe minimal online instructional quality. Using this QM rubric, an experienced faculty member may choose to participate in a peer review process to evaluate the quality of his or her online course design. In general, the instructional strategies prescribe the need to align measurable learning objectives to the presentation of course materials, the practice of new content, and the assessment of learning outcomes. In addition, instructional strategies include the grading and interaction strategies identified as essential faculty tasks, but more commonly referred to in terms of preparation to teach, facilitation of the learning, and communication with students. Although it is new territory for many online community college faculty, they are learning the essential tasks and pedagogical skills through trial-and-error. As noted, the technological skills are not as important as the instructional assumptions and strategies associated with the pedagogical approach, which are shaped by the field of instructional design.

Online Course Production Model

How an online course is produced has a tremendous impact on what knowledge and which skills the faculty member will need to master, whether those skills are related to new technologies or instructional design. The type of production can increase, change, or eliminate the need for acquiring new skills and knowledge and reposition the faculty member's traditional place in the teaching and learning process. In any case, the type of production model in which the faculty member works helps indicate which skills and knowledge he or she will need to be successful.

When a faculty member performs all of the essential tasks in an online course, the professional role can be described as tightly bundled; in other words, the faculty member maintains control over the how the work is performed, who performs it, and how the quality is determined. He or she shoulders the full weight and responsibility for performing these tasks. When the essential tasks are performed by others or by using technologies as a substitute for faculty interaction, the professional role becomes unbundled. Online course production models exist on a continuum from bundled tasks done by the faculty member to highly unbundled tasks performed by others. This helps to share the load the faculty bears but also tends to decrease the need for mastery of all of the essential skills and tasks.

The production of online courses in community colleges can be classified as three models: craft, collegial, and virtual assembly line (Smith and Rhoades, 2006). In each model, the knowledge and skills needed to accomplish the essential tasks are completed in similar and contrasting ways. Depending on the model, the faculty member may or may not need to perform the essential task and therefore may or may not need to acquire the corresponding skill set.

Craft Production.   Generally the craft model is characterized by a single faculty member working as the primary producer of all the essential tasks. In the model, faculty members work collaboratively in teams to accomplish the essential tasks. The full unbundling of the faculty role happens in the virtual assembly line model as the essential online course tasks are segmented, specialized, produced, and delivered by other professionals and semiprofessionals. The faculty member may perform some or none of the essential tasks needed to create and deliver an online course.

In the craft model, the faculty role is highly bundled. The same faculty member performs all of aspects of the online production process: course design, content, development, delivery, grading, interaction, improvement, and advising. This model produces mastery in all of the skill sets over time. Craft model faculty members do their own research and development on what will be best for their online course in terms of pedagogy and technology. They learn instructional and graphic design principles. They become skilled at putting courses into the course management system and figuring out how to make that system work with the student information systems. They tackle testing and proctoring issues, constantly improve their online courses, and conduct the advising tasks for their students. No essential task is ignored.

Because the tasks are performed by a single faculty member and are highly bundled, the result is a greater impetus for that faculty to increase professional knowledge and skills development. He or she tends to be a full-time faculty member in the craft model. This is the default online course production model. Course management systems are implicitly or explicitly structured around the assumptions and characteristics found in this way of accomplishing these essential tasks. Most online community college courses fit into the craft model.

Collegial Production.   Much like the craft model, the collegial model for online production uses the professional and collegial relationships of faculty to accomplish all of the essential tasks and processes needed to create and deliver the online course. These faculty members work within their departments and through organizational structures across campus e-learning committees and in conjunction with teaching and learning centers. Informal collegial networks provide the support to create and collaborate on courses.

Much like the traditional guild model, new or curious online faculty work with colleagues who are experienced in the use of the course management systems and the types of pedagogical approaches most effective as determined by the technology or media and their own experience. Professional relationships, where there are informal mentoring and apprenticeships, often are developed. The new faculty member analyzes the structure, format, and instructional strategies found in previous online courses and then consults with the experienced faculty member to understand the rationale and history behind the syllabus, lessons, assignments, exams, and so forth.

In the collegial model, full-time faculty members work together to complete all of the tasks of course production, with minor assistance from other personnel, mostly for technology support and access to college servers. While colleagues may specialize in certain essential tasks, all members are expected eventually to master all of the tasks as well. For example, one faculty member may work on the production of the assessment instruments for the grading tasks, while another works on putting the course lessons into the course management system to accomplish the development tasks. The collegial model increases the technology skills and professional expertise during all phases of the production process. Because the tasks may be performed by one or more faculty members, including part-time faculty members, the collegial model can be described as being partially unbundled. This model emerges as college departments seek to increase the number of online courses available. Each faculty member builds on another's skills and knowledge by creating a synergistic online course that is then shared by colleagues with their students.

Virtual Assembly Line Production.   Whenever the virtual assembly line model exists, the faculty role becomes highly unbundled. Essential tasks, functions, and processes become the domain of part-time faculty or other nonfaculty professionals. A team assembles virtually, in many cases never having face-to-face or synchronous meetings with all team members present. The full-time faculty team member may be asked to take care of the content tasks as a "content specialist" or "subject matter expert." Course design is done by instructional designers, and content can be created by part-time faculty members hired for that specific task. The placement of the course materials into the course management system, the coding, and other development tasks are performed by technicians who specialize in those skills. The delivery is assisted by other technicians found in the information technology or distance learning course office. Grading and interaction may be done by a faculty member, but such tasks are most likely performed by part-time faculty or other graders who may not be faculty. Improvement tasks fall to instructional designers, and advising tasks are done by advisors in the student services or student enrollment offices.

In this model, the entire production process, starting with course design, is directed and coordinated by instructional designers who may or may not report to faculty. The model uses a temporary workforce in an inverse ratio to full-time faculty where few full-time faculty take part in the essential tasks, and large numbers of part-time faculty and managed professionals do the work in their place. The result is a complex organizational structure, highly specialized and bureaucratic in nature. Because the tasks are performed by a number of people—instructional designers, graphic designers, Web specialists, advisors, and so forth—the virtual assembly line model is highly unbundled. Technology is for the instructional technologists or IT department, and pedagogical issues are for the instructional designers. Faculty do not have the same need or impetus to increase their professional knowledge and skills development in the virtual assembly line model. In fact, it may be in the interest of the faculty to move to the heart of their professional domain and concentrate on the subject matter of their discipline to preserve their remaining unique skills and knowledge. This model can be found in colleges with large numbers of online courses where there has been a strategic effort to offer online courses in the attempt to reach economies of scale.

Rebundling Essential Tasks.   Of the three models of online course production, the bundled craft model is the default mode as well as the preferred state for faculty members. By controlling the production of essential tasks, faculty members maintain their professional role. Given the opportunity, they will try to rebundle their professional role despite the production model. Both a sense of responsibility to complete essential tasks associated with the faculty member's sense of professional identity and the desire to meet perceived student needs are primary drivers for faculty members to rebundle their roles in online community college courses (Smith, 2008).

Rebundling the essential tasks helps faculty members determine who accomplishes the work and how the essential tasks will be organized and accomplished, and it makes the determination of how and when online courses will be offered and by whom. This rebundling becomes possible for the faculty member through involvement in all of the essential online course tasks and mastering the skill sets associated with the tasks. The extent to which a faculty member does not possess the skill sets for essential online course tasks, the greater the likelihood is that he or she will run into a great deal of frustration, like that expressed by the faculty member who said that she would "never do it again."

Alternatively, the tasks will be performed by others, such as instructional designers and Web specialists. These nonfaculty members then gain the skill sets while the faculty member, if not gaining more knowledge and expertise in some way, becomes marginalized, deskilled, and unbundled. Clearly there are trade-offs between lightening the load and supporting faculty members and creating new relationships that make the faculty member more dependent on other specialists in order to teach online classes. Rebundling is a natural tendency because of the desire on the part of faculty to maintain control over the work they perform.

Suggestions for Practice

As part of the ongoing professional development in an online community college setting, faculty members, administrators, and online course staff should identify the model of course production supported at their college. The strategic placement of teaching online courses should be examined within the context of the college's future trajectory. With this understanding, the essential tasks that faculty members will need to perform become apparent. Next, the institutional support systems and personnel, such as instructional technologists and instructional and Web designers, should be identified. Faculty members should also conduct a self-inventory of their own skill set, ideally with the assistance of experienced online faculty members. Learning and mastering the technologies associated with a course management system cannot be avoided. The level of mastery would be highly determined by the type of course production model used at the community college. Familiarity with the course management systems and other online technologies for the presentation of content and interaction with students can be obtained through many educational opportunities—again, depending on the course production model. Finally, faculty members, administrators, and all of those involved in online courses should approach the acquisition of these skills in a systematic and patient manner. Great faculty can become even greater as they become familiar with this new professional territory, its tasks, and required skills.

Online courses are growing at a rapid pace in all of higher education, and especially in community colleges. Over the past decade, creating and delivering online courses has also led to new and essential tasks that faculty must accomplish, and new skill sets accompany the essential tasks. These new skills incorporate the selection and application of new technologies and new instructional assumptions and strategies. The online course production model used to create and deliver online courses, and the efforts by faculty members to control and rebundle their role, influence which faculty skills will be required to be successful as online faculty. This will transform the skills, the role, and the community college faculty as a profession.

References

Abbott, A. *The System of Professions: An Essay on the Division of Expert Labor.* Chicago: University of Chicago Press. 1988.

Allen, I. E., & Seaman, J. *Staying the Course: Online Education in the United States, 2008.* Needham, Mass.: Sloan Consortium, 2008.

Boettcher, J. V. "How Much Does It Cost to Put a Course Online? It All Depends." In C. F. Martin, J. Finkelstein, F. I. Jewett, and B. W. Scholz (eds.), *Dollars, Distance, and Online Education: The New Economics of College Teaching and Learning.* Phoenix, Ariz.: American Council on Education and the Oryx Press, 2000.

Clift, E. "I'll Never Do It Again." *Chronicle of Higher Education,* May 29, 2009. Retrieved June 11, 2009, from http://chronicle.com/free/v55/i38/38a03302.htm.

Daniel, J. S. *Mega Universities and Knowledge Media.* London: Kogan Page, 1996.

Goodyear, P., and others, "Competences for Online Teaching: A Special Report." *Educational Technology Research and Development,* 2001, 49(1), 65-72.

Hughes, E. C. *On Work, Race, and the Social Imagination.* Chicago: University of Chicago Press, 1994.

Instructional Technology Council. *2008 Distance Education Survey Results: Tracking the Impact of eLearning at Community Colleges.* Washington, D.C.: Instructional Technology Council, 2009.

Jewett, F. I. "A Framework for the Comparative Analysis of the Costs of Classroom Instruction Vis-à-Vis Distributed Instruction." In C. Frances, F. I. Jewitt, and B. W. Scholz (eds.), *Dollars, Distance, and Online Education: The New Economics of College Teaching and Learning.* Phoenix, Ariz.: Oryx Press, 2000.

Kim, K., and Bonk, C. J. "The Future of Online Teaching and Learning in Higher Education: The Survey Says . . ." *EDUCAUSE Quarterly,* 2006, 4, pp. 22-30.

Krause, E. A. *Death of the Guilds: Professions, States, and the Advance of Capitalism, 1930 to the Present.* New Haven, Conn.: Yale University Press, 1996.

Lee, J. L., & Hirumi, A. "Analysis of Essential Skills and Knowledge for Teaching Online." Association for Educational Communications and Technology, Chicago, Oct. 19-23, 2004. ED485021.

Levin, J. S., Kater, S., & Wagoner, R. L. *Community College Faculty: At Work in the New Economy.* New York: Palgrave Macmillan, 2006.

Paulson, K. "Reconfiguring Faculty Roles for Virtual Settings." *Journal of Higher Education,* 2002, 73(1), pp. 123-140.

Rhoades, G. *Managed Professionals: Unionized Faculty and Restructuring Academic Labor.* Albany, N.Y.: SUNY Press, 1998.

Slaughter, S., and Rhoades, G. *Academic Capitalism and the New Economy: Markets, State and Higher Education.* Baltimore, Md.: Johns Hopkins University Press, 2004.

Smith, V. "The Unbundling and Rebundling of the Faculty Role in E-Learning Community College Courses." Unpublished doctoral dissertation, University of Arizona, 2008.

Smith, V., and Rhoades, G. "Community College Faculty and Web-Based Classes." *Thought and Action,* 2006, 22, 97-110.

Troutt, W. E. "Unbundling Instruction: Opportunity for Community Colleges." *Issues and Trends in American Education,* 1979, 56, 253-259.

Twigg, C. A. "Affordability in Higher Education." 2003. Retrieved June 11, 2009 from http://search.epnet.com/direct.asp?an=32Y0974019514&db=f5h.

Twigg, C. A. "Is Technology a Silver Bullet?" *EDUCOM Review,* 1996, 31(2). Retrieved June 11, 2009 from http://net.educause.edu/apps/er/review/reviewArticles/31228.html

Wang, W. K. S. "The Unbundling of Higher Education." *Duke Law Journal, 53,* 55-60, 1975.

VERNON C. SMITH *is vice president of academic affairs at Rio Salado College in Tempe, Arizona, one of the Maricopa Community Colleges.*

NEW DIRECTIONS FOR COMMUNITY COLLEGES • DOI: 10.1002/cc

As online learning continues to grow, so do the free or nearly free Web 2.0 and emerging online learning technologies available to faculty and students. This chapter explores the implementation process and corresponding considerations of adapting such tools for teaching and learning. Issues addressed include copyright, intellectual property, support, and privacy.

6

Web 2.0 and Emerging Technologies in Online Learning

Veronica Diaz

The number of instructional offerings in higher education that are online and blended (in which a portion of the course is delivered online and a portion is delivered face-to-face with reduced seat time), including courses and programs, continues to grow exponentially. More than 3.9 million students took at least one online course during the fall 2008 term, a 12 percent increase over the number reported the previous year, with the bulk of that growth in community colleges (Allen and Seaman, 2008). Institutions are becoming more focused and experienced with e-learning delivery options and are learning how to support learners and faculty members more effectively in these environments. As a result, colleges and universities are still pursuing some strategic benefits of technology-mediated instruction, including greater student access, an increased rate of degree completion, and improved student retention, especially in the areas of continuing and professional education (Allen and Seaman, 2007).

Alongside the growth of e-learning, higher education has witnessed the explosion of Web 2.0 and other emerging technologies (Sclater, 2008). Web 2.0, which refers to the vast array of socially oriented Web-based tools that are free or nearly free, has represented a transition from institutionally provided to freely available technology tools. For instance, in the past, community colleges may have offered enrolled students server space to host a personal Web site or store instructional content. Now students can use Google for those purposes and others before, during, and after they are

NEW DIRECTIONS FOR COMMUNITY COLLEGES, no. 150, Summer 2010 © 2010 Wiley Periodicals, Inc.
Published online in Wiley InterScience (www.interscience.wiley.com) • DOI: 10.1002/cc.405

57

affiliated with any institution. Although Web 2.0 tools offer many instructional opportunities, their emergence has widened the gap between faculty and student use of technology and has also presented some support and faculty development difficulties. This chapter addresses the numerous teaching and learning opportunities and challenges that institutions face in adopting and implementing emerging technologies into their e-learning programs.

What Are Web 2.0 or Emerging Web-Based Technologies?

Web 2.0 and emerging technologies such as blogs, wikis, social networking sites, photo- and video-sharing sites, and folksonomies (a system of classification) enhance e-learning programs. A recent study (Salaway, Caruso, and Ellison, 2008) of undergraduate student use of information technology (IT) found that between 17 and 47 percent of learners across all institutional types were engaged in the use of Web 2.0 tools, including wikis, blogs, and social bookmarking (see Table 6.1). While some learners reported using the tools for entertainment or socializing, others reported use connected with instructional activities, such as blogging while studying abroad.

In many ways, Web 2.0 tools support a trend that began with the emergence of the Internet: a shift away from large organizational control of the instructional function toward the individual user, both faculty member and learner. These emerging technologies, not necessarily created for higher education consumption, support and require individual creativity and autonomy, and foster the growing trend toward user-generated content and knowledge in a way that many institutionally developed products do not. Part of the rapid proliferation of these tools in higher education can be attributed to their ease of use and the opportunity they present for low- or

Table 6.1.   Learner Use of Web 2.0 Tools

Web 2.0 Activity	Percentage of Learners Engaged
Contribute content to photo or video Websites (Flickr, YouTube)	46.6%
Contribute content to wikis (Wikipedia, course wiki)	38.2
Contribute content to blogs	34.1
Podcasts	29.1
Webcasts	25.0
Social bookmark or tagging (del.icio.us, etc.)	16.7

Source: Salaway, Caruso, and Nelson (2008),
Note: N = 27,317. Learners reported monthly frequency of use for all tools. The median frequency of use is calculated only for learners engaged in an activity.

no-cost instructional innovation in a time of shrinking budgets. Faculty members and learners no longer need to wait for a learning or course management system to develop and implement a tool, an institution to purchase a license to use images, or a streaming media server because many of these needs can now be met externally through a variety of Web 2.0 tools.

Although thousands of these tools exist in the virtual world, several issues exist in implementing them in an instructional environment. Although implementation is not without its challenges, some important reasons may justify doing so. A recent report (Partnership for 21st Century Skills, 2008) identifies several areas relevant and critical to a service economy: creativity and innovation, critical thinking and problem solving, and communication and collaboration. Over the past several decades, our manufacturing-based industrial economy has shifted to a service economy driven by information, knowledge, and innovation. Furthermore, to be effective in the twenty-first century, citizens and workers must be able to exhibit a range of functional and critical thinking skills such as literacy in information; media; and information, communications, and technology (ICT). The demand for these new skills can be connected to some of the affordances of Web 2.0 tools: active engagement, knowledge creation, independent learning, reflection, and innovation.

Many faculty members correctly assert that while today's students enter institutions having had some exposure to Web 2.0 tools such as Facebook, they lack an awareness of how those tools can be used for learning. Faculty members may also have noticed that entering students have a heightened comfort level with the type of digital environment that has the potential to be connected to learning. For instance, students tend to have a greater tolerance for figuring out, troubleshooting, or experimenting with technology. They can deal with a trial-and-error approach to tool use and change in general and often have had a broad exposure to a variety of different Web-based software and hardware tools. All of these affordances translate into valuable skills and abilities that can be leveraged in the learning experience: problem solving, critical thinking, and the ability to use a menu of learning options. And finally, the burden to support students in the use of new technologies is reduced, making it possible to have experimentation and innovation in learning. As with other skills that students bring to the learning experience, developing the skill to use emerging technologies for instruction merits the effort that is required to integrate them into learning.

One challenge is the sheer volume of tools that exist with no simple way to narrow the search process for a faculty member looking to select and implement one. This is especially true for the novice user who may not be familiar with the Web 2.0 vernacular. Generally Web 2.0 tools can be classified into a few categories: communicative, collaborative, documentative, generative, and interactive. Table 6.2 can serve as a preliminary organizer of the instructional purpose that these tools may serve.

NEW DIRECTIONS FOR COMMUNITY COLLEGES • DOI: 10.1002/cc

Table 6.2.   Web 2.0 Tool Classifications

Web 2.0 Tool Type	Instructional Purpose	Examples
Communicative	To share ideas, information, and creations	Blogs Audio blogs Video blogs IM-type tools Podcasts Video chat
Collaborative	To work with others for a specific purpose in a shared work area	Editing and writing tools Virtual communities of practice Wikis
Documentative	To collect or present evidence of experiences, thinking over time, productions, and so on	Blogs Video blogs E-portfolios Wikis
Generative	To create something new that can be seen or used by others	Mashups Virtual communities of practice Virtual learning worlds
Interactive	To exchange information, ideas, resources, materials	Learning objectives Social bookmarking Virtual communities of practice Virtual worlds

Web 2.0 tools were not primarily designed for higher education and certainly not as learning or course management systems (LCMSs), but some faculty members have identified tools that can address many of the commercial LMS functions and serve as portals to other tools otherwise unavailable. For instance, Netvibes is a free Web service that aggregates various media sources and online services such as blogs, news, weather, videos, photos, social networks, and e-mail. Another tool is Ning, which allows the integration of various social networking tools, including a forum, blog, and calendar.

In the past few years, colleges have experienced many changes in course management systems. Some systems have been acquired by other vendors, as is the case with WebCT and Angel. The increasing cost of commercial products has prompted many institutions to consider open source systems, which usually are implemented with the assistance of third-party software development entities that support the development and modification of such systems. The LMS landscape has become more diverse in response to the growing number of available tools and systems. Not only does each of these options have very different associated cost structures, but, perhaps more important, each has a broad range of control options. Table 6.3 illustrates ways in which the three most common systems vary in their ability to be modified from their original configuration or setup and

**Table 6.3.   Learning and Course Management System:
Adaptability and Support Considerations**

Product Type	Control/Modification Ability	Tool Support Level	User Support Level
Commercial product (Desire2Learn, Blackboard)	Low/low	Low	High
Open source product (Sakai, Moodle)	High/high	High	High
Web 2.0 product (Netvibes, Ning)	Low/high	Low	Low

the degree of support that the tool itself as well as both faculty and student users need.

As evidenced in Table 6.3, there are significant pros and cons inherent in the more established course support options, perhaps shedding some light as to why Web 2.0 tools are becoming more popular in the higher education community. Despite their many benefits, however, these tools present some institutional challenges as well. In the past, faculty members and learners had few, if any, choices on how to create and manage a virtual learning environment. When the Internet first became available, early adopters created HTML Web pages, but many others used nothing at all. Later, the emergence of the learning and course management system enabled less technologically savvy faculty members to create a virtual presence with few or no technology skills. Web 2.0 tools, many of which are primarily used by experimenters and early adopters, place control of the learning environment with the individual user, both faculty member and learner. These tools present a diverse menu of teaching and learning options that are under the user's complete control. Institutionally selected and developed products can sometimes alienate and confine the user to limited instructional environments and possibilities.

Perhaps the most striking opportunity that Web 2.0 tools offer is for learners, who have traditionally not participated in any decisions relating to their learning environment. Many tools empower and enable students to choose, virtually create, collaborate, share, network, and publicize as they see fit, independent of an institution. For instance, by using the vast array of Google products, students can work on documents collaboratively with other students, create personal Web sites, store content, and manage e-mail and calendars. Another reason that students are increasingly exploring and using Web 2.0 tools and products is the portability that these options afford them. Over the course of their education, students will produce a significant amount of content, much of which they will likely want to reference while in their next educational courses, programs, institutions, or places of employment. Many proprietary tools allow content to be easily exported or removed, making the use of a nonaffiliated or supported tool a desirable option.

Web 2.0 Implementation Considerations

When a decision is made to use Web 2.0 technologies, it is important that colleges consider issues associated with implementation such as intellectual property, privacy, local hosting, data collection, and faculty training.

Web 2.0 and Intellectual Property.   The rise of user-generated content and the ability to conduct teaching and learning functions outside the institutional purview raises the importance of corresponding intellectual property issues. Intellectual property policies before the advent of e-learning typically addressed ownership of traditionally copyrighted materials such as books, articles, and other conventional academic products. In an online environment, course materials take on a greater presence than in a traditional one. In a physical classroom, an instructor can meet with students and have no materials beyond class notes and a text, yet he or she can still deliver the course. In cyberspace, this becomes more difficult. Course materials begin to embody or encapsulate many of the processes of the physical classroom. In the digital setting, it is possible to unbundle course materials and realize the potential profit for each one separately or together as a package. Authority over instructional products and responsibility regarding development and maintenance spurred institutions to revisit existing intellectual property policies, especially those that did not address important emerging questions and conflicts in these areas.

Instructional control and production processes, especially in the online environment, have been transferred to the faculty and learners and away from the institution. As teaching and learning activity increased with the growth in hybrid and online delivery models, intellectual property policies changed to address and capture the new area of instructional product development. Online and blended learning delivery models have already changed the way faculty members and institutions regard ownership and control of instructional products, but the emergence and proliferation of Web 2.0 tools will surely spur a second wave of institutional intellectual property policy reviews.

In the mid- to late 1990s, institutions began to revise their intellectual property policies for several reasons. With the rise of e-learning, new markets emerged for digital instructional products, many that had no value or did not exist in the past, prompting colleges and universities to either develop or revise policy sections dealing with copyrighted materials, including software and instructional technologies. As a result of those changes, many of today's policies contain language that differentiates between digital and nondigital property and contains specific and substantial rights over these now economically viable products. Higher education institutions have generally advanced claims to the faculty's copyrightable intellectual products under certain conditions, which are commonly found in policy language. Some of this language originates in copyright legislation, such as "work for hire," which affords the employer ownership of the property created, and "within the scope of employment," which again effectively enables the institution to claim ownership of the property created. Other language addresses "use of institutional resources" or "substantial use of institutional resources," which furthers an institution's case for ownership and control. In fact, the often-substantial institutional resource contribution (instructional designers, programmers, and support staff) necessary to participate in some forms of e-learning is recognized and specifically mentioned in policy language. The intersection of intellectual property rights, specifically the area of copyright, and technology in higher education is the realm of e-learning, including distance education, digital repositories, and electronic courseware products. The emergence of Web 2.0 tools is likely to spur institutions to once again reexamine their intellectual property policies to ensure that they are addressing development in an online environment.

Web 2.0 and Privacy.   An often-overlooked consideration regarding the use of Web 2.0 tools involves privacy. The Family Educational Rights and Privacy Act (FERPA) is the federal law that protects the privacy of student educational records. Institutional interpretations of what constitutes a "student's educational record" vary, but many consider any work related to a course or program of study to fall into this category. Although FERPA does not prohibit faculty members from using Web 2.0 and other publicly available tools, some guidelines do apply. One way to address FERPA is to include a statement in the syllabus such as this one:

This [insert name of technology tool] is for academic use of [insert name of course], [insert term/year]. It is open to the public for the purpose of sharing our work with the larger Internet community. To use this [insert name of technology tool] responsibly, please observe all laws and college policy that are incorporated into the [insert institution's policy name and location here]. Some specific aspects of law and policy that must be adhered to include prohibitions against copyright infringement, plagiarism, harassment or interference with the underlying technical code of this software.

As a student using this [insert name of technology tool], certain rights accrue to you. Any original work that you make tangible belongs to you as a matter of copyright law. You also have a right to the privacy of your educational records as a matter of federal law. Your contributions to this [insert name of technology tool] constitute an educational record. By contributing to this [insert name of technology tool], and not taking other options available to you in this course equivalent to this assignment that would not be posted publicly on the Internet and not available for the editing by others, you consent to the collaborative use of this material as well as to the disclosure of it in this course and potentially for the use of future courses.

Including a statement such as this, reviewing it with students, and providing alternatives to the use of Web 2.0 tools is good practice and likely sufficient in addressing any FERPA issues that may arise.

Local Implementation of Web 2.0 Tools. Locally hosting and implementing Web 2.0 tools outside a course management system is an option that provides the desired functionality with institutional support, privacy, and control. Penn State's Education Technology Services for instance, supports locally hosted blogs, wikis, and podcasting services for teaching and learning. Arizona State University's implementation of Google Apps is another example where learners have access to iGoogle, Google's portal, in addition to applications including e-mail, calendar, chat, sites, and Google Docs.

Another possibility is to support learner use of Web 2.0 tools while still using institutionally supported systems for course management. For instance, learners could be encouraged to use blogs to document their academic experience or study-abroad experiences, or to reflect on course work. Or they could use wikis to support team-based learning or collaborative project work or to track and display their academic accomplishments with an e-portfolio. Alternatively, social bookmarking and RSS feeds could be used to support student research.

Use of Data in Implementation Decisions. Before adopting any learning technology tool, Web 2.0 and others, institutions should collect data about their students and their students' use of technology. The EDUCAUSE Center for Applied Research Study of Undergraduate Students and Information Technology is a good example of a survey instrument that can be used or adapted to assess students' ownership of, use of, and skill level with information technology, information technology and the learning and academic experience, and their use of Web 2.0 tools and other emerging technologies. Considering the increasingly greater budget portions that institutions are allocating to the support of learning and information technologies, it is critical to evaluate on an annual basis what existing tools and services, as well as future tools and services, need to be supported.

Faculty Development and Quality Assurance. A final but critical consideration in selecting and supporting the use of Web 2.0 tools in any learning environment is to have a well-developed institutional faculty development program that includes some mechanism for quality assurance. Encouraging or requiring faculty members to complete some training before delivering a technology-mediated course, especially as it relates to the use and role of technology, is an important first step. If an instructor has taught in an online or hybrid environment for many years, she or he might be encouraged to participate in some form of course review process. An example of a widely used quality assurance process is Quality Matters, a faculty-centered peer review process designed to improve the quality of online courses and components. This rubric, as well as other similar locally developed tools, is designed to offer faculty members a systematic and comprehensive approach by which to review their courses and check for things such as the clarity of learning objectives, assessment and measurement tools, resources and materials used to support the learner, learner engagement, and technology used to support desired learning outcomes. Implementing quality assurance can be especially important in supporting faculty members to use Web 2.0 tools in a way that is aligned with their course objectives and closely connected to achieving student learning outcomes.

Web 2.0 Implementation: Moving Forward

Several items should be considered in making the decision whether and how to support Web 2.0 tools. The following steps could serve as a guide in forming implementation decisions:

1. Adopt an institution-wide data collection initiative addressing students and their use of technology for learning.
2. Assemble a local institutional team including individuals from the faculty, instructional technology or design, information technology, the student body, and the administration to collect information and make decisions involving support for faculty members and students around current instructional practice, Web 2.0 tools, and other emerging technologies.
3. Before launching initiatives, consult with and involve individuals who can advise and offer support around policy issues relating to intellectual property, FERPA, and copyright laws.
4. Periodically explore alternative solutions that can support the faculty and learners in the use of innovative and emerging learning technologies that exist within or can be integrated into an existing LMS product or by locally hosting an externally available Web 2.0 tool.

Technology and information continue to proliferate and raise costs in ways that make it challenging for faculty members and institutions to keep up. For these and many other reasons, it is important to strategically select and support the technologies that are closely related to the college's core challenges and missions: student access, retention, and learning. Regularly assessing the technology tools and initiatives that exist will lead to a better understanding of the value of our investments and adjust our resources accordingly.

References

Allen, I. E., and Seaman, J. *Online Nation: Five Years of Growth in Online Learning.* Needham, Mass.: Sloan Consortium, 2007.
Allen, I. E., and Seaman, J. *Staying the Course: Online Education in the United States, 2008.* Needham, Mass.: Sloan Consortium, 2008.

Partnership for 21st Century Skills. *21st Century Skills, Education and Competitiveness: A Resource and Policy Guide*. Tucson, Ariz.: Partnership for 21st Century Skills, 2008. Retrieved Dec. 5, 2009, from http://www.21stcenturyskills.org/documents/21st_century_skills_education_and_competitiveness_guide.pdf.

Salaway, G., Caruso, J. B., and Nelson, M. R. *The ECAR Center for Applied Research Study of Undergraduate Students and Information Technology*. Boulder, Colo.: EDUCAUSE Center for Applied Research, 2008. Retrieved Dec. 5, 2009, from http://www.educause.edu/ers0808/135156.

Sclater, N. *Web 2.0, Personal Learning Environments, and the Future of Learning Management Systems*. Boulder, Colo.: EDUCAUSE Center for Applied Research, 2008. Retrieved Dec. 5, 2009, from http://www.educause.edu/ecar.

VERONICA DIAZ *is associate director of the EDUCAUSE Learning Initiative in Washington, D.C.*

NEW DIRECTIONS FOR COMMUNITY COLLEGES • DOI: 10.1002/cc

This chapter explores the potential of social networking sites for increasing student engagement for distance education learners. The authors present a modified student engagement model with a focus on the integration of technology, specifically social networking sites for community college distance education learners. The chapter concludes with challenges and implications for integrating social networking sites in the classroom and on the college level.

7

Potential of Social Networking Sites for Distance Education Student Engagement

Jaime Lester, Michael Perini

[The] new era embraces the . . . perception that high quality education is shaped by changes in the characteristics of student learners and the ways in which they use new technologies to exchange information. One thing is clear: the convergence of social networking technologies and a new "always on" pedagogy is rapidly changing the face of education.

D. E. Baird and M. Fisher (2005–2006)

The focus of this chapter is the student groups that enroll in community college distance education formats and the need to consider new models and practices for student engagement. Community college students are particularly important in a discussion of distance education because they comprise the majority of students enrolled in distance and online courses (Allen and Seaman, 2008). More specifically, this chapter argues for an extension of the student engagement model to include an interaction with social network sites.

Social networking sites (SNSs) designed to connect individuals to each other by affinity groups are becoming more widespread. In fact, a recent EDUCAUSE Center for Applied Research (ECAR) survey (Salaway and others, 2007), which polled community college and four-year students, found that 98 percent of students owned a computer and 75.8 percent owned laptop computers. The study further notes that wireless connection use

New Directions for Community Colleges, no. 150, Summer 2010 © 2010 Wiley Periodicals, Inc.
Published online in Wiley InterScience (www.interscience.wiley.com) • DOI: 10.1002/cc.406

increased from 12.4 percent in 2005 to 24 percent in 2007, with a similar increase of smartphone use from 1.2 percent in 2005 to 10.1 percent in 2007. In terms of SNSs, Junco and Mastrodicasa (2007) found that 68.5 percent of students surveyed had an SNS profile, though they estimated that due to newer avenues of accessibility, that number likely is higher today. Use of Facebook in particular is high among college students. Over 85 percent of all college students are reported as Facebook users (Arrington, 2005), and college students spend on average 6.2 hours per week on Facebook (Martinez Aleman and Wartman, 2008).

Social networking sites are virtual spaces that build virtual communities through sharing experiences, communicating personal information, and connecting to friends. While there are many social networking sites (among them are Bebo, LunarStorm, Mixi, and Orkut), the most popular in the United States are Facebook, MySpace, and Twitter. These sites are becoming a primary means of communication and have moved private lives into a public forum (Katz and Rice, 2002). The connection between SNSs and higher education is strong, particularly with Facebook. Initially introduced only for users who had a college or university e-mail address, Facebook expanded later to the general public (Junco and Mastrodicasa, 2007), and traditional-aged college students (ages eighteen to twenty-four) specifically use Facebook more than MySpace or other SNSs (Salaway and others, 2007). A University of Michigan study noted that over 99.5 percent of the students had Facebook profiles (Matney, Borland, and Cope, 2008); therefore, we focus primarily on Facebook in this chapter, but recognize that the recommendations could apply to many other SNSs. Also, generation gaps do exist in SNS use, with more traditionally aged students using SNS regularly. National statistics report that almost half (43 percent) of community college students are under the age of twenty-one (American Association of Community Colleges, 2008).

The extensive use of SNSs and their reliance on higher education audiences make them essential to consider as ways to promote student engagement. Moreover, these sites provide a social outlet for students despite the barriers of distance, and it has been shown that interaction with friends at school is significantly higher for students who spend more time on these sites (Higher Education Research Institute, 2007). SNSs are an "easier way to connect in a disconnected world" (Junco and Mastrodicasa, 2007).

In this chapter, we review the research on student engagement and the specific ways that distance education students engage in higher education. Because these students are often not on campus, they do not fall under the traditional paradigm of engagement that includes faculty-student interaction and active and collaborative learning in a face-to-face classroom (Kuh, Kinzie, Schuh, & Whitt, 2005; Tinto, 1987). We continue with a discussion of SNSs, how these new technologies alter student engagement, and ways they can be used to further engage distance learners. Much of the literature on SNSs examines students at four-year universities, yet represents the best and most recent literature on the subject. The chapter concludes with recommendations for research and practice.

Before we begin, we add a caveat here to address the wide variation in the definition of a distance education student. While some students enroll in distance education and face-to-face courses simultaneously and could fall under the definition of a distance education learner, we are focusing on students who spend entire semesters with all online courses. Also, we do not limit our definition to synchronous study ("same time" participation in the class) or asynchronous study (student participation to occur at the leisure of the student).

Student Engagement Models and Distance Education Learners

Decades of research on student engagement unpack the means through which students successfully complete a postsecondary degree or certificate (Astin, 1993; Kuh, Kinzie, Schuh, and Whitt, 2005; Pascarella and Terenzini, 1991, 2005). Student engagement focuses not on what students bring to college (such as motivation and academic preparation), but what students do in college and how student behaviors, opportunities, and environments mediate college retention and graduation (Kuh and others, 2005). Kuh and others (2005) provide the most comprehensive model of student engagement, which includes academic challenge, student-faculty interaction, and active and collaborative learning. *Academic challenge* entails the "amount of time and effort students devote to (1) studying and other academic work, (2) preparing for class, (3) reading assigned and other books, and (4) writing" (Kuh, Kinzie, Schuh, and Whitt, 2005, p. 45) and produces challenges that present themselves through the entire academic experience, from orientation to graduation. *Student-faculty interaction* refers to interactions inside and outside the classroom, such as discussions about career plans, working on research projects, and discussing course readings outside the classroom. *Active and collaborative learning* involves both the individual student's application of learned measures in varied situations, along with the interaction with colleagues in order to solve problems and tasks (Kuh, Kinzie, Schuh, and Whitt, 2005). This involves classroom response and discussion as well as group work.

The robust model provided by Kuh and others (2005) as well as the foundational work of Astin (1993), Tinto (1987), and Pascarella and Terenzini (1991, 2005) primarily applies to traditional students in four-year universities, not to community college distance education learners. Rather, to understand the ways in which distance education learners engage in college, we need to consider use of technology, integration into the campus community (a modified look at faculty to student interaction), and student-to-student communication.

In the online community, the faculty own a significant role in distance education (Dzuban, Shea, and Arbaugh, 2005). Often faculty are the only connection that distance education learners have with the college. While some courses may require peer-to-peer interaction for group assignments, others do not require direct student interaction. Thus, faculty e-mail or other electronic-mediated responsiveness may be the only form of student engagement that takes place. Yet studies have found that students enrolled in online courses often did not receive accurate or complete feedback from instructors or received incomplete responses (Bambara, Harbour, Davies, and Athey, 2009; Rovai, 2001). High-quality and engaged teaching, online or in person, is critical to student engagement.

Separate from faculty-to-student interaction but related to active and collaborative learning is student-to-student engagement. Distance education students do not enter brick-and-mortar classrooms with the opportunities to meet fellow students, share ideas and concerns, and increase their social and professional networks. Rather, these students must reach out to fellow students or be assigned collaborative learning. Bambara, Harbour, Davies, and Athey (2009) found that students had little to no contact with each other. They did not hear other perspectives on issues and were unable to learn from each other. Distance education students who did reach out to others in electronic correspondence were more successful (Bambara, Harbour, Davies, and Athey, 2009), and those who successfully negotiated group activities online found that their abilities to use technology were enhanced (Askov and Simpson, 2002). Furthermore, when such learning occurs, distance education students were more likely to experience beneficial diverse and multicultural educational experiences (Rovai, Ponton, and Baker, 2008). Active and collaborative learning also require mediation by faculty interaction. Students in distance education courses report that discussion boards are rarely used and do not offer meaningful faculty interaction (Bambara and others, 2009). SNSs offer ways to bridge communication gaps and facilitate interface inside the classroom and out.

Another area of student engagement that is absent from research on traditional student populations is the impact of technology infrastructure and knowledge of technology. Distance education students rely solely on properly operating technology to deliver the course curriculum. Distance learners often encounter issues with technology ranging from course management systems such as Blackboard and WebCT that are inoperable to difficulty in navigating the course management systems and an inability to access the course content due to password failure (Bambara, Harbour, Davies, and Athey, 2009). If substantial problems exist within the design of the technology, the issue "will inevitably contribute to the initial general lack of [student] engagement . . . in subsequent e-learning and the learning experience as a whole" (Loke, 2005). However, this presumes that all distance learners possess the same academic resources. The United States suffers from a digital divide with unequal access to high-speed Internet and personal computers among underrepresented populations and in rural areas (Rovai, Ponton, and Baker, 2008).

Given the context for distance education students, engagement in postsecondary education likely differs and their circumstances are not wholly met by traditional models of student engagement. We propose that distance education student engagement must include the use of technology, integration, and an adapted view of social engagement using such technology. Social networking sites have the potential to mediate each of these areas of engagement.

Incorporation of Web 2.0 Technologies in Distance Education Student Engagement

The first way in which SNSs can promote student engagement for distance education learners is by connecting students with the administration. "Facebook puts a massive amount of information and communication power at a student's fingertips, making it possibly the ultimate synthesis of student-relevant data" (Heiberger and Harper, 2008, p.20). The live interaction available on SNSs through instant messaging and easy-to-update content creates a sense of a supportive campus environment. Through the ability to interact easily with campus-based services and faculty across the university, students are connected to a network—a specified group that shares information. In addition, researchers have found a connection between students' ability to stay connected with a community and their use of SNSs (Ellison, Steinfield, and Lampe, 2007). When students engage with these sites, they are able to stay informed and continue to identify with that group. Community colleges can promote identification with the campus through continued interaction on Facebook or other such sites. Furthermore, a variety of student services might use SNSs to address perceived gaps in administrative support, specifically in "non-academic responsibilities" (Community College Survey of Student Engagement, 2008). This is particularly important because online students often feel disconnected from the campus and require alternative methods for engagement.

While e-mail contact also serves as a method to increase student and faculty interaction (Kuh and others, 2005), SNSs have the potential to connect students to each other in a more meaningful way. E-mail has text with the addition of emoticons (the combination of colons, semicolons, and parentheses to make faces). Social networking sites offer places to post pictures, video, and profiles with information on one's job, preferences, interests, and the like. Message boards are also included where individuals can post information about a person or just send a message (this is an alternative to the e-mail feature, which is also commonly part of SNSs). Student personnel can also use SNSs to send personal messages and help students receive information in a timely manner. Learning more about faculty and fellow students though these opportunities can provide more meaningful interactions.

NEW DIRECTIONS FOR COMMUNITY COLLEGES • DOI: 10.1002/cc

Active and collaborative learning is a hallmark of student engagement. In traditional classrooms and college campuses, active and collaborative learning includes asking questions in class, making class presentations, working with other students on projects, and discussing course concepts and readings with others (Kuh and others, 2005). Distance educators attempt to simulate these activities through the use of discussion boards, e-mail, group project assignments, and other methods to promote collaboration in the virtual classroom. Social networking sites can also create opportunities for active and collaborative learning through the use of communicative applications. For example, instructors could ask students to respond to short questions using the wall function on Facebook, be available through the instant messaging function to other students, and form smaller groups to engage in collaborative projects in a nonspecifically academic program such as Blackboard. Using SNSs has an advantage to other course management systems because the messaging is immediate, students can network with each other, and many students are logged on to an SNS several hours each day.

Also, SNSs can increase the time that a student is engaged in learning by making the learning appear to be social or a part of regular activities, such as updating his or her status on Facebook. Research notes that students who engage in active and collaborative learning regularly are more likely to attain their educational goals (Hijzen, Boekaerts, and Vedder, 2007; Leithwood and Jantzi, 2000). Students of the millennial generation have grown up with the Internet and have integrated SNSs into their daily social activities, so using these Web sites for educational purposes may combine their uses and promote more time spent in collaborative learning.

Challenges of Adopting Social Networking Sites

The promise of SNSs for student engagement is not without challenges. Some students are apprehensive about interacting with administration on these sites which are typically used as places of social action and not as places to conduct school-related business (Watson, Smith, and Driver, 2006). A similar challenge related to the social dynamic of SNSs occurs when faculty and campus staff attempt to communicate using these sites. Miller and Jensen (2007) found that library professionals who did not actively seek interaction with students did not experience high levels of communication with the students through an SNS. These professionals had to seek out students and promote SNSs as a means for communicating about academic needs and concerns. Moreover, some professors are finding difficulty maintaining a line of proper interaction with students and faculty on these Web sites (Young, 2002). Campuses that seek to engage students using SNSs may consider alternative profiles and groups separate from students' socially oriented profiles.

NEW DIRECTIONS FOR COMMUNITY COLLEGES • DOI: 10.1002/cc

Another challenge concerns integration of technology into pedagogy. A criticism of rapid adoption of technologies in the classroom concerns suitability and appropriate integration into curriculum. More often than not, faculty introduce a new piece of technology and do not use it for active and collaborative learning. Therefore, institutions must introduce technological conditions only if the instructional faculty retain a firm understanding of its applications. Wholesale changes to classroom requirements could leave instructors not fully adapted to distance education, resulting in poor student experience and extended time requirements for faculty (Young, 2002). Therefore, integration of SNSs needs to become a seamless part of the curriculum and not just an additional means for communication. Professional development programs and mentoring among faculty to share successful integration of these sites are just two examples of ways to overcome these challenges and capitalize on the power of social networking in the classroom.

Technology infrastructure and legal matters also pose challenges for using SNSs to engage distance learners. Colleges and universities struggle with the integration of third-party Web-based innovations because the information is stored outside secure campus servers. In addition, more online communication creates a need for additional storage capacity on campus servers. When a message is sent from Facebook, an e-mail is sent to the profile owner, thus creating more e-mails for campus servers to store. Infrastructure and legal concerns collide when considering Family Educational Rights and Privacy Act (FERPA) regulations. Transmitting personal information in an online environment without security protocols may be too risky for some colleges to consider, and alternative arrangements, such as the development of an SNS created and stored locally on a campus server, are just too costly. Community colleges need to evaluate their level of comfort in risk management before engaging students on a Facebook page and create documents to guide instructors and staff in what information is appropriate to share.

Recommendations for Research and Practice

The promise of SNSs to engage distance education students is great. We recommend several new lines of inquiry for empirically testing new models of student engagement based on student use of technology. First, more research is needed that targets distance education students. The assumption of students who enroll in distance education is that they already engage in computer technologies. Do students who use computers for instruction also engage in other computer-mediated social networking behaviors? We need to know if these learners have profiles on SNSs and how often they are on a computer. Also, are these sites perceived as only social spaces? Are the sites enhancing or detracting from social engagement for distance students? Does the active integration of SNSs integrate two spheres, social and academic, that students perceive as incompatible?

Second, the scholarship of teaching and learning has yet to engage in experiments that implement various forms of online activities within the context of distance education courses. Do students who engage in SNSs have better outcomes, such as higher grades and better retention? Most important, national surveys that measure student engagement do not disaggregate or sample distance education students and are just beginning to integrate questions about technology. More measures on national surveys will help to begin unraveling the potential of SNSs on student engagement. Surveys such as the National Study of Student Engagement and Community College Survey of Student Engagement should continue considering new items, as they are in forthcoming surveys, about use of SNSs, computer access, and the integration of SNSs in course curriculum and student services.

Third, Martinez Aleman and Wartman (2008) have a recent book on the impact of SNSs on student identity. Their findings examine the ways in which students develop their individual identities through technological means such as these sites. We need to examine in more detail and with additional student groups the impact of the Internet on student engagement on college campuses. While this chapter addresses only distance education students, undergraduate students across postsecondary education interact in large numbers in an online environment. Anecdotally, we see undergraduates who complete group assignments, meet classmates, and communicate with friends exclusively online in SNSs. What are the implications for our models of student engagement when students engage in virtual communication the majority of the time?

Practitioners have many opportunities to engage distance learners though SNSs. For example, many colleges across the country have engaged Facebook by establishing a college-sanctioned Facebook page. Students are able to "friend" the college and connect to other students and student services. Specific student services and student groups may also create their own Facebook page, advertise on the main university page, or provide online opportunities for updates on events and connecting to services such as academic advising. If successful, these departments might bridge interaction gaps that persist in the academic sectors between students and administrators (National Study of Student Engagement, 2007). New technologies that are connected to Facebook, such as Twitter, offer even more ways to keep students apprised of campus events, both online and face-to-face. This may be particularly appealing to rural community colleges, which often serve as sites and centers of community events.

Another recommendation for community colleges is to consider promoting the use of SNSs by integrating these sites within the course curriculum. Faculty could promote interaction by creating group or fan pages in Facebook, developing Twitter accounts to update peers and faculty on their course progress, or creating blogs to promote discussion and commentary on course subjects. While learning has been accessed primarily

NEW DIRECTIONS FOR COMMUNITY COLLEGES • DOI: 10.1002/cc

through writing assignments, shorter updates via Twitter and the use of Web links, video, and other wikis can show a degree of cognitive complexity and an acceptance of multiple learning styles. Assessment of learning does not need to occur in traditional formats, especially when students are engaging in an online format.

Integrating new technologies does require professional development for faculty and staff, review of the legality of content on profile pages, dissemination of information to guide faculty and staff on ways to adhere to FERPA guidelines, and a review of technology infrastructure. While distance education learners can benefit from and potentially engage more in the college campus, thus leading to higher student outcomes, the benefits cannot be realized unless the campus is able to manage the environment, prevent the illegal distribution of student information, and use SNSs to promote active and collaborative learning.

Conclusion

Social networking sites have much promise for engaging distance education learners, a group that has little to no physical connection with the community college. Distance education students can benefit from more meaningful interactions with faculty and fellow students, keep students actively engaging with the campus, and provide more access to campus services, thereby creating a more supportive culture for distance learners. Yet applying and using Web 2.0 technologies for student engagement requires understanding how and why students are using specific forms of technology (Heiberger and Harper, 2008; Guidry, 2008) and adapting to the changes before they become superseded by future innovations (Fox and Madden, 2005; Salas and Alexander, 2008; Timm and Junco, 2008). Community colleges, individual departments, and instructors must review and overcome the challenge to experiment with these new and low-cost technologies to engage one of the largest student populations: distance learners.

References

Allen, I. E., and Seaman, J. *Staying the Course: Online Education in the United States, 2008.* Needham, Mass.: Sloan Consortium, 2008.

American Association of Community Colleges. "State by State Profile." 2008. Retrieved Aug. 3, 2009, from http://www2.aacc.nche.edu/research/index.htm.

Arrington, M. "85 Percent of College Students Use Facebook." 2005. Retrieved June 12, 2009, from http://www.techcrunch.com/2005/09/07/85-of-college-students-use-facebook/.

Askov, E. N., and Simpson, M. "Penn State's Online Adult Education M.Ed. Degree on the World Campus." *Quarterly Review of Distance Education,* 2002, 3(3), 283-294.

Astin, A. W. *What Matters in College: Four Critical Years Revisited.* San Francisco: Jossey-Bass, 1993.

Baird, D. E., and Fisher, M. "Neomillennial User Experience Design Strategies: Utilizing Social Networking Media to Support 'Always On' Learning Styles." *Journal of Educational Technology Systems,* 2005-2006, 34(1), 5-32.

Bambara, C. S., Harbour, C. P., Davies, T. G., and Athey, S. "Delicate Engagement: The Lived Experience of Community College Students Enrolled in High-Risk Online Courses." *Community College Review,* 2009, *36,* 219-238.

Community College Survey of Student Engagement (CCSSE). *High Expectations and High Support.* Austin, TX: The University of Texas at Austin, Community College Leadership Program, 2008.

Dziuban, C., Shea, P., and Arbaugh, J. B. "Faculty Roles and Satisfaction in Asynchronous Learning Networks." In S. R. Hiltz and R. Goldman. (eds.), *Learning Together Online: Research on Asynchronous Learning Networks.* Mahwah, N.J.: Erlbaum, 2005.

Ellison, N. B., Steinfield, C., and Lampe, C. "The Benefits of Facebook 'Friends': Social Capital and College Students' Use of Online Social Network Sites." *Journal of Computer-Mediated Communication,* 2007, *12*(4), article 1. Retrieved from http://jcmc.indiana.edu/vol12/issue4/ellison.html.

Fox, S., and Madden, M. "Generations Online, 2005." Retrieved June 12, 2009, from http://www.pewInternet.org/~/media//Files/Reports/2006/PIP_Generations_Memo.pdf.pdf.

Guidry, K. R. "Exploding a Myth: Student Affairs' Historical Relationship with Technology." *Student Affairs On-Line,* 2008, *9*(2). Retrieved from http://www.studentaffairs.com/ejournal/Winter_2008/UndergraduateStudentUseofTechnology.html

Heiberger, G., and Harper, R. "Have You Facebooked Astin Lately? Using Technology to Increase Student Involvement." In R. Junco and D. M. Timm (eds.), *Using Emerging Technologies to Enhance Student Engagement.* New Directions for Student Services, no. 124. San Francisco: Jossey-Bass, 2008.

Higher Education Research Institute. *Results of the 2007-2008 Faculty Survey Conducted by the Higher Education Research Institute.* 2008. Retrieved from http://www.ipfw.edu/vcaa/assessment/PDFs/2007-2008%20HERI%20FACUTY%20SURVEY%20FINAL%20RESULTS.pdf

Hijzen, D., Boekaerts, M., and Vedder, P. "Exploring the Links Between Students' Engagement in Cooperative Learning, Their Goal Preferences and Appraisals of Instructional Conditions in the Classroom." *Learning and Instruction,* 2007, *17,* 673-687.

Junco, R., and Mastrodicasa, J. *Connecting the Net.Generation.* Washington, D.C.: National Association of Student Personnel Administrators, 2007.

Katz, J. E. and Rice, R. E. *Social Consequences of Internet Use: Access, Involvement, and Interaction.* Cambridge, Mass.: MIT Press, 2002.

Kuh, G. D., Kinzie, J., Schuh, J. H., and Whitt, E. J. *Assessing Conditions to Enhance Educational Effectiveness: The Inventory for Student Engagement and Success.* San Francisco: Jossey-Bass, 2005.

Kuh, G. D., and others. *Student Success in College: Creating Conditions That Matter.* San Francisco: Jossey-Bass, 2005.

Leithwood, K., and Jantzi, D. "The Effects of Transformational Leadership on Organizational Conditions and Student Engagement with School." *Journal of Educational Administration,* 2000, *38*(2), 112-129.

Loke, J.C.F. "Blackboard: A Virtual Learning Environment or Administrative Tool?" *E-Journal of Instructional Science and Technology,* 2005, *8*(1). Retrieved from http://www.ascilite.org.au/ajet/e-jist/docs/vol8_no1/content2.htm

Martinez Aleman, A. M., and Wartman, K. L. *Online Social Networking on Campus: Understanding What Matters in Student Culture.* New York: Routledge, 2008.

Matney, M., Borland, K., and Cope, M. (2008, March 10). *Facebook, blogs, and other electronic communication: How students construct new environments through social networking sites.* Program presented at the NASPA Annual Conference. Boston, MA.

Miller, S. E., and Jensen, L. A. "Connecting and Communicating with Students on Facebook." *Computers in Libraries,* 2007, *27*(8), 18-22.

National Study of Student Engagement. *Experiences that Matter: Enhancing Student Learning and Success, Annual Report 2007.* Bloomington, IN: Indiana University Bloomington, Center for Postsecondary Research.

Pascarella, E., and Terenzini, P. *How College Affects Students: Findings and Insights from Twenty Years of Research.* San Francisco: Jossey-Bass, 1991.

Pascarella, E., and Terenzini, P. *How College Affects Students: A Third Decade of Research.* San Francisco: Jossey-Bass, 2005.

Rovai, A. P. "Building Classroom Community at a Distance: A Case Study." *Educational Technology Research and Development,* 2001, 49(4), 33-48.

Rovai, A. P., Ponton, M. K., and Baker, J. D. *Distance Learning in Higher Education: A Programmatic Approach to Planning, Design, Instruction, Evaluation, and Accreditation.* New York: Teachers College Press, 2008.

Salas, G., and Alexander, J. "Technology for Institutional Enrollment, Communication, and Student Success." In R. Junco and D. M. Timm (eds.), *Using Emerging Technologies to Enhance Student Engagement.* New Directions for Student Services, no. 124. San Francisco: Jossey-Bass, 2008.

Salaway, G., and others. *The ECAR Study of Undergraduate Students and Information Technology, 2006.* Washington, D.C.: EDUCAUSE, 2007.

Timm, D. M., and Junco, R. "Beyond the Horizon." In R. Junco and D. M. Timm (eds.), *Using Emerging Technologies to Enhance Student Engagement.* New Directions for Student Services, no. 124. San Francisco: Jossey-Bass, 2008.

Tinto, V. *Leaving College: Rethinking the Causes and Cures of Student Attrition.* Chicago: University of Chicago Press, 1987.

Watson S. W., Smith, Z., and Driver, J. "Alcohol, Sex and Illegal Activities: An Analysis of Selected Facebook Central Photos in Fifty States." 2006. Retrieved from ERIC database. (ED493049)

Young, P. "The 24-Hour Professor: Online Teaching Redefines Faculty Members' Schedules, Duties, and Relationships with Students." *Chronicle of Higher Education,* May 3, 2002, A31-A33 .

JAIME LESTER *is an assistant professor of higher education in the College of Humanities and Social Science at George Mason University in Fairfax, Virginia.*

MICHAEL PERINI *is a graduate student in the higher education program at George Mason University in Fairfax, Virginia.*

The authors explore the processes involved in moving to online student services at community colleges, relate success stories, and address the challenges involved.

8

Online Student Services at the Community College

Anne M. Hornak, Kayeri Akweks, Madeline Jeffs

The use of online technology in community colleges has exploded over the past two decades, changing the manner in which services need to be delivered to students. This chapter examines online student services at the community college, beginning with a brief historical overview of the growth of online student services. We then explore opportunities and challenges presented by new technology; discuss the design, planning, implementation, and assessment phases of a student services technology plan; and conclude with a presentation of emerging trends and challenges.

Historical Overview

Student services professionals are integral to the success and persistence of community college students (Ender, Chand, and Thornton, 1996), and the integration of technology into our everyday lives has fundamentally changed how they do their jobs. Technology has become an invaluable tool in providing services to students and has created incredible opportunities and practices as they also present new challenges. Community colleges must provide online access to student services in order to remain competitive. Technology should "improve service to students, from recruitment through graduation and beyond" (McLean, 2007). The development of a student services technology plan is critical to the success of online services and should be part of every college's enrollment management strategy (McLean, 2007).

New Directions for Community Colleges, no. 150, Summer 2010 © 2010 Wiley Periodicals, Inc.
Published online in Wiley InterScience (www.interscience.wiley.com) • DOI: 10.1002/cc.407

Opportunities

Technology has significantly changed the manner in which students interact with colleges. According to a 2006 Cornell University survey (Erickson and others, 2007) of 885 public and private two-year degree-granting institutions, "Over 90 percent of the colleges surveyed offer online access to college catalogs, class schedules and online courses. Between 80 percent and 90 percent also offer financial aid applications, admissions applications and course registration online. Six out of ten offered bursar billing online" (p. 3). Some institutions reported offering only online access to services such as the college catalogue, course registration, class schedules, and financial aid applications. Institutions that used to rely on face-to-face interactions, standard mail, campus announcements, printed media, or automatic phone messaging systems now use Web sites, e-mail, instant messaging and chat functions, streaming video, social networking Web sites, and multiple other virtual venues to communicate with students.

Community colleges are serving an increasing proportion of students under the age of twenty-four—the millennial generation. The majority of these students not only are tech-savvy but feel technologically entitled. They expect services instantly and on demand. The have been described in this way: "Millennials are the iGeneration—always wired, always plugged in and always communicating" (Berger, 2006, para. 2). For most of these students, computer-based technologies are a way of life. We must reconsider not only the services we provide to this generation but also "the means by which these services are delivered" (Lowery, 2004, p. 95). Traditional delivery venues may not be the most effective means for this generation. It is important that colleges understand the services to be delivered, as well as the ways in which delivery will take place.

Online services are not just for students enrolled in online courses; they can enhance the collegiate experience for all students, particularly those who have infrequently accessed college resources in the past or may prefer to access help and information on the Web. Colleges use online services to attract students; improve outreach, recruitment, and student retention; provide new ways of interacting with financial aid, academic advising, and personal counseling; build a sense of community; and create new avenues of campuswide communication, such as emergency notification systems and Web-based calendars.

Before they even apply, prospective students judge colleges on their Web sites. The college Web site has become the first door of student entry. Thus, colleges should give considerable attention to site development to ensure a professional image and consistency of message, format, and style, and should avoid dazzling effects at the expense of actual student needs for accurate and timely information and ease of maneuverability.

Many colleges use customer relationship model software for outreach and recruiting. Colleges track and categorize student interactions, creating profiles for each student. Student services practitioners then use the student profiles to tailor communications, services, and programs to individual student interests and needs.

Most students and their families find the financial aid process complex and daunting. In order to stay true to the community college mission of open access, students must be able to access financial aid information without needing to visit the campus. Resources such as financial aid FAQs address routine queries and significantly decrease repetitive staff contact.

Academic advising can provide a wide range of online services to students, including e-mail advising and advisor chatrooms that allow either live or asynchronous discussions of student questions. Integrating Web applications with the college's student information system allows students to access their own academic records.

Some services, due to their sensitive nature, present added challenges when offered on the Web. As with academic advising, most personal counseling for students has historically been provided in face-to-face interactions. Now that students may also receive additional support in the form of chatrooms and online support groups, colleges must address new issues of Internet protocol, confidentiality, privacy, and security.

Research over the past two decades shows that building a sense of community is an important factor in maximizing student success (Ender, Chand, and Thornton, 1996). The majority of community college students commute rather than live on or near campus, and online students may never visit campus. Student services professionals must assist these students with establishing and maintaining ongoing relationships with college faculty and staff and in fostering connections within the college. Data from the 2003 National Study of Student Engagement (NSSE) suggested that technology that is used effectively can improve student engagement (Young, 2003). For online and commuter students, technology provides an opportunity to develop virtual communities and fosters a sense of belonging to the institution, which may increase retention and completion rates (Crawley, 2004).

Challenges

The generational divide—an average thirty-year difference (Stephens, 2007)—that is often noted between students and faculty is also present with staff. Millennials often show an ease and facility with technology, but faculty, student services practitioners, and staff who do not see the benefit of these modalities or feel technologically adept may be daunted by the explosion of new technological opportunities.

Many student services professionals also find it difficult to accept using technology to interact with students in areas where they are used to face-to-face contact. For instance, there is often a disconnect between the institution's increased online academic offerings and the rigidity with which student services personnel adhere to the need for on-campus orientation programs. An online orientation can use different formats and time lines in information distribution to address different learning styles and information needs. These same arguments can be made with regard to academic advising.

It will take a cultural shift within institutions to realize the benefits that technology can bring to the services and programs provided to students. Staff already proficient in current technologies may take the lead in restructuring how to share information, engage students, and provide services.

Although many students are proficient and highly skilled in technology, others, especially at community colleges, may not be as familiar with or have access to various forms of technology. Martin and King (2009) view this dilemma as another "barrier that is often detrimental to [the success and persistence] of our disadvantaged students." The digital divide requires careful analysis of the range of student knowledge and familiarity with online technology during online planning, implementation, and assessment stages. Continuous training in information literacy and online skills is essential for faculty and staff if they are expected to use technology effectively.

It also is important to recognize that 60 percent of students with disabilities who attend public colleges or universities are at two-year institutions (Erickson and others, 2007). In the Cornell University study of Web-based student processes, thirty community colleges were evaluated regarding their compliance with Section 508 of the Vocational Rehabilitation Act of 1973 Web accessibility standards. The study found no institutional compliance in financial aid, academic programs, and class schedule information pages, and admissions application pages were only minimally compliant. Web accessibility policies within community colleges are a good first step but are not sufficient to ensure that all users, including those with disabilities, can use and access Web content.

Designing Services

The design of online student services should consider the multiple forms of technology that students use. Access is no longer limited to personal computers (Moneta, 2005). The majority of community college students are proficient in tools that include handheld devices, podcasts, Internet, e-mail, instant messaging, and social networking (Junco and Cole-Avent, 2005).

More than 85 percent of students report frequent use of a personal computer (Hurtado & Pryor, 2007), so colleges must provide online services that are fully functional and effective. Students should have the ability to save and reopen various online applications as well as track the receipt and processing of their transactions. Ease of use and navigation of interactive services, such as providing a secure, single log-in so that students do not have to enter and exit with each discrete interaction, must also be taken into ongoing consideration.

Planning

Planning should begin with an assessment of the essential services students need in order to be successful. This should be done with a cross-campus team that includes professionals from information technology, student services, and academic affairs. Students should also be part of the conversation and planning, as some may be far more comfortable and up to date in the technological environment than staff are. Once essential services are identified, the team should discuss the urgency of online access and the resources necessary to complete the task. It is not necessary or desirable to move everything to the Web all at once; colleges should instead first identify the essential services that can be easily accessed using the Web. Next, a time line should be established to determine when services would be moved and become operational virtually. For example, it may be determined that an online orientation is essential for students, and so the plan to go online with orientation becomes a top priority. Conversely, it may be determined that paying tuition through a secure site is not a top priority, so resources are not mobilized at that time toward that effort. Priorities on the list should be determined by the college's needs, as well as the resources available to put services online. The long-term goal should be to put all student services online (Shea, 2005), but not at the expense of quality. As much as possible, the online environment should allow students to navigate without staff assistance and without difficulty.

Implementation

The next step in moving toward Web-based student services is implementation, which needs to be accomplished with care and concern for quality and access. The implementation plan should begin with an analysis of the technical support available within the college. What hardware and software standards does the service require? What levels of technology support does the campus provide for internal and external assistance? What types of security safeguards does the service require? What level of access should be provided? What is the expertise of students using the online student services? Many other questions may arise as the implementation process and plan are carried out. Implementation frequently occurs in stages. As the college learns how to use technology to support and educate students, an ongoing assessment plan needs to be built into the long-term strategy.

Assessment

Assessment is essential to understanding the effectiveness of online student services. The assessment process should be an ongoing loop that begins with the development of the goals of the services. The assessment plan should have benchmarks that measure the sophistication of the online services and how they are meeting the needs of the students. Modifications should be expected and ongoing as the technology and needs of students change.

We recommend that the technology plan include an in-house pilot component that tests the site before students gain access. "User testing is a critical first step in creating websites and design based on actual user perspectives, rather than institutional perspectives" (Erickson and others, 2007, p. 6). Having a pilot site ensures that bugs are identified and problems resolved before going live. This can be accomplished with a static site as well as a dummy site that is behind the live site.

The assessment plan should be inclusive of the departments that are responsible for not only the information technology functions but also the student services units that deliver the services. All departments should be involved from the planning and implementation stages through the assessment plan. The assessment process needs to be fully detailed at the onset, and each time a component is assessed, the findings should be disseminated and problematic issues addressed. The assessment process is essential to continuous quality improvement, as it will drive changes in processes and upgrades in software and equipment.

Future of Online Student Services

Millennial students expect colleges tailored to their interests. They expect customization and active and collaborative learning. They also expect learning to occur at high speed with instant feedback and payoffs. This population, with values formed by the Internet, will be a growing proportion of the total enrollment (Seppanen and Prince, 2009).

The future of student services will be dramatically affected by the transition of all traditional services into various combinations of online services and face-to-face interaction. Students will continue to view their world and education through the lens of technology as a means to expand connectivity and improve personal convenience. Individual student-centered processes and interfaces will become specialized, personalized, and socially networked. Students will unilaterally determine the timing of the information flows that meet their individual needs. They may prefer to use one central source for all online student service interfaces. This source will have intelligence programming that enhances its capabilities at a rate consistent with each student's growing technological ability to manage it. Customization of tools will be the norm. Using specialized technology, students will be able to manage their own academic progress with understanding of the possibilities and opportunities available to them.

The effects of the Web on a student's worldview are profound. Students see the world as dynamic, fragmented, and saturated with ever-shifting information, capital, and social and environmental struggles. They use technology to solve complex problems drawing on multiple skills and face an expanding interdependent world community. Mobile online student services will continue to get more and more dynamic student usage. Smartphones and the future generations of telecommunications will become the principal interface for students and online student services. Online student services technologies will channel student access to the institution's multiple touch points into a constructed student life pathway that meets each student's personalized needs.

Democratic equalization of students and online student services staff will lead to new styles of lateral communication and marketing because of the Internet. Content service professionals will drive system, performance, and assessment design. Service levels will expand over time through the use of technology-based "service counters" that track questions, answers, and technology difficulties into databases of help strategies. The construction of technology-led pathways will drive design of student services practices. Training and retraining of staff will become part of the ongoing work structure because of constant technology changes. Technology itself will demand new business models for all staff functions.

Costs for keeping current with new technologies will be progressively mitigated through systemwide purchasing, which will require new governance rules and new business models (Washington State Board for Community and Technical Colleges, 2008). Online student services will take advantage of semantic Web data technologies to offer students and staff interactive pooled data. Business intelligence based on Web analytics in real time will inform the administration's business decisions and business processes. Green sustainability practices will touch all areas of higher education, including the powering of online student services through sustainable energy solutions. All student services, including online student services, will be subject to progressively more rigorous assessments, measurement, and standards.

Student leadership will demand greater input in institutional planning and decision making about technology that is important to their lives. Interaction with students will happen within their personalized, customized, technology-based mobile technology. Online student services will develop ongoing student course mapping for a wide variety of career opportunities. This expanded service will greatly contribute to students' abilities to plan their collegiate experience to meet their long-term career goals.

Conclusion

Effective delivery of online student services can increase access, convenience, and timeliness of information distribution and improve student-staff interaction. It can also assist students in developing self-management skills. Online services will continue to evolve, "creating decision support systems that offer students a variety of opportunities for self-help and that customize services for individual students" (Krauth and Carbajal, 2001).

A student services technology plan is critical to the success of online services and should be part of every college's enrollment management strategy (McLean, 2007). Community colleges must prepare for the further integration of new and yet-to-be-developed technologies into both curricula and online student services and stay abreast of the rapid changes that will come with ongoing staff and faculty enrichment courses, while also providing opportunities for students less familiar with technology to catch up. A well-designed online student services plan will increase institutional organization and efficiency and empower students to navigate both their academic experience and the world beyond confidently.

References

Berger, S. "Generation M." *State Press Magazine*, Oct. 16, 2006. Retrieved Sept. 11, 2009, from www.statepress.com/issues/2006/10/16/arts/698227.

Crawley, A. "Online Student Services Benefit All Students." *Student Affairs Online*, 2004, 5(1). Retrieved Sept. 1, 2009, from http://studentaffairs.com/ejournal/Winter_2004/index.html.

Ender, K. L., Chand, S., and Thornton, J. S. "Student Services in the Community College: Promoting Student Success and Learning." In S. C. Ender, F. B. Newton, and R. B. Caple (eds.), *Contributing to Learning: The Role of Student Affairs*. New Directions for Student Services, no. 75. San Francisco: Jossey-Bass, 1996.

Erickson, W., and others. *Web Based Student Processes at Community Colleges: Removing Barriers to Access*. Ithaca, N.Y.: Cornell University, June 2007.

Hurtado, S. & Pryor, J. H. (2007). Looking at the past, shaping the future: Getting to know our students for the past 40 years. Presentation at *NASPA/ACPA Joint Conference*, Orlando, FL.

Junco, R., and Cole-Avent, G. A. "An Introduction to Technologies Commonly Used by College Students." In K. Kruger (ed.), *Technology in Student Services: Supporting Student Learning and Services*. New Directions for Student Services, no. 112. San Francisco: Jossey-Bass, 2005.

Krauth, B., and Carbajal, J. *Western Cooperative for Educational Telecommunications Guide to Developing Online Student Services*. 2001. Retrieved Aug. 12, 2009, from http://www.wcet.info/2.0/.

Lowery, J. W. "Student Affairs for a New Generation." In M. D. Coomes and R. DeBard (eds.), *Serving the Millennial Generation*. New Directions for Student Services, no. 106. San Francisco: Jossey-Bass, 2004.

Martin III, Q., and King, D. B. "Access and Integration: Meeting the Technological Needs of our Students." *iJournal: Insight into Student Services*, 2009, 21. Retrieved May 31, 2009, from http://www.ijournalccc.com/articles/issue_21/martin-king.

McLean, M. "Making the Case for Student Lifecycle Management." *Campus Technology*, 2007. Retrieved May 31, 2009, from http://campustechnology.com/articles/49336.

Moneta, L. "Technology and Student Affairs: Redux." In K. Kruger (ed.), *Technology in Student Services: Supporting Student Learning and Services*. New Directions for Student Services, no. 112. San Francisco: Jossey-Bass, 2005.

Seppanen, L., and Prince, D. *Major Trends to Impact College in the Next Two Decades*. Washington State Board of Community and Technical Colleges Mission Study Task Force. 2009.

Shea, P. A. "Serving Students Online: Enhancing Their Learning Experience." In K. Kruger (ed.), *Technology in Student Services: Supporting Student Learning and Services*. New Directions for Student Services, no. 112. San Francisco: Jossey-Bass, 2005.

Stephens, D. *Literature Review: Technology Investment Needs of Students and Faculty at Community Colleges*. Olympia, Wash.: Washington State Board for Community and Technical Colleges, 2007.

Washington State Board of Community and Technical Colleges. *Strategic Technology Plan for Washington State Community and Technical Colleges*. Olympia, WA: Author, 2008.

Young, J. R. "Student Engagement in Learning Varies Significantly by Major, Survey Finds." *Chronicle of Higher Education*, Nov. 14, 2003, A37.

ANNE M. HORNAK *is assistant professor of educational leadership at Central Michigan University in Mount Pleasant, Michigan.*

KAYERI AKWEKS *is a student services policy associate at the State Board for Community and Technical Colleges in Olympia, Washington.*

MADELINE JEFFS *is vice president for student services at Columbia Basin College in Pasco, Washington.*

9

This chapter discusses the notion of quality in online education and attempts to find some commonality among the numerous existing definitions.

Approaching Common Ground: Defining Quality in Online Education

Regina L. Garza Mitchell

The notion of quality in regard to teaching and learning has always been highly debatable. Is it best measured by qualitative or quantitative measures? Summative or formative assessments? Comparative or independent studies? As someone deeply involved with online education for many years, I continue to seek definitive answers. During my time as director of distance education for a medium-sized community college, I focused on quantitative data, namely, comparisons of retention rates and student grades between online and on-site classes. Those numbers illustrated that online courses had a higher attrition rate than on-site courses and that there was no significant difference between the final grades of students in either set of courses, though the online students tended to have slightly higher grades. Now I am skeptical that numbers alone gauge the quality of online courses.

Yet quality remains a primary concern of everyone involved with online education. Quality assessment still relies on measuring outcomes often using completion rates of courses and programs, which we know may not be the best measure for any community college program, or through comparisons of grades or attrition of online and face-to-face sections. An underlying assumption in comparing online and face-to-face courses builds on the ideal that face-to-face courses are inherently better. Online courses are given legitimacy if they are able to measure up to existing, sometimes outdated, standards and expectations set for face-to-face courses.

NEW DIRECTIONS FOR COMMUNITY COLLEGES, no. 150, Summer 2010 © 2010 Wiley Periodicals, Inc.
Published online in Wiley InterScience (www.interscience.wiley.com) • DOI: 10.1002/cc.408

This chapter explores the notion of quality in regard to online education and assumptions that contribute to the idea of lesser quality in online education, and it seeks to find commonalities that may be used to define and measure the quality of online education.

How Is Quality Defined?

The definition of quality is nebulous at best. The conception of what makes a "good" course depends on who defines the parameters. Existing measures of the quality of online education can be separated into four categories, all of which may be used at a college to assess its own program: stakeholder perceptions, quantifiable elements, course design elements, and external standards.

Reports on stakeholder perceptions can be either quantitative or qualitative and rely on feedback from students, instructors, and others directly involved with online education. These reports are similar to satisfaction surveys that some colleges carry out. Stakeholders report back on whether they perceive courses, instructors, and programs as being of high quality. Reports of this type usually comprise survey data and can be useful in determining how stakeholders define quality.

Quantifiable elements such as grades or test scores or retention and graduation rates are commonly used to determine the quality of online courses. Quantifiable elements are those most likely required by boards of trustees, state and national organizations, and accrediting agencies. Quantifiable elements are often used to comparatively study the quality of online courses. For example, grades or test scores of an online course may be compared to those of a face-to-face section. These comparative studies stem from the "no significant difference" studies conducted during the 1990s (Russell, 1999). These studies sought to determine the differences between the quality of online and face-to-face courses through various comparisons. Studies of this type are still conducted and relied on to justify the quality of online courses. However, two key issues remain. One important consideration is that these studies do not always compare the same things and do not account for other factors that may have an impact on quality, such as instructional methodology, student comfort and preparation, and instructor comfort and preparation (Meyer, 2002). Another consideration is the underlying assumption that face-to-face courses remain the standard of comparison to which online courses are expected to measure up, though there is no proof that face-to-face courses adhere to quality standards (McDonald, 2002; Sener, 2004).

Course design elements are often used to define and determine the quality of online courses during the design phase. The premise is that if a course is designed properly, student learning should occur and the course will be of high quality. This conceptualization aligns with traditional notions of teaching where the content defines the learning (Barr and Tagg,

NEW DIRECTIONS FOR COMMUNITY COLLEGES • DOI: 10.1002/cc

1995). Course design elements may be measured separately through checks of technology elements used in a course, discussion elements included in a course, or review of content areas. In examinations of course design, an assumption is that unilateral course design benefits all students taking the course. This should not imply that there is not a focus on student learning. On the contrary, elements of course design are often intended to appeal to a variety of student learning types that are defined by an organization, group, or college. However, it is acceptable practice at many institutions that an online course is developed by one person and then reused by others who teach the course. Course instructors may have some room in adjusting the course to fit student needs, depending on the college's policies. This type of course design involving a single designer or design team was intended to increase the quality of courses by incorporating instructional design principles. However, it may wind up with an adverse impact on student learning if instructors are not provided the latitude to adjust a course to fit student needs and instructor comfort.

The fourth category for defining quality stems from standards developed by various external groups and organizations. These organizations include accrediting agencies, lawmakers, colleges, and groups such as Quality Matters and the Sloan Consortium. Quality Matters has developed standards that a number of community colleges use, and many other colleges have adopted similar standards. The standards are based on accepted principles of good instructional design and require a review of courses by no fewer than three instructors from within and outside the discipline. The Sloan Consortium's (Bourne and Moore, 2001) quality standards encompass online education as a whole and focus on learning effectiveness, cost-effectiveness, student support services, and faculty and student satisfaction.

An emerging system that attempts to gauge quality for learners is Transparency by Design, an offshoot of the Western Telecommunications Educational Consortium. The main difference with Transparency by Design is that it uses common measures, intended to be transparent in nature, to assess student engagement, general education, learning outcomes, and satisfaction, but assessment for degree programs varies by institution (Lederman, 2009). Transparency by Design also encourages colleges to be transparent about how they assess quality by sharing that information publicly. These agencies have come up with means of assessing online courses that have agreed-on standards used by colleges and within disciplines.

This brief overview highlights various means for assessing the quality of online courses and programs. Obviously there are as many ways of assessing quality as there are of defining it. In order for colleges to best assess the quality of their online courses and programs, they should first define what they mean by quality and strive to assess both online and face-to-face courses accordingly.

NEW DIRECTIONS FOR COMMUNITY COLLEGES • DOI: 10.1002/cc

Assumptions About Learning

Formal education at the postsecondary level has changed little over the years. The ideal remains that education consists of one or more experts in the role of teacher or instructor who imparts his or her expertise to students enrolled in a course. Although alternative definitions of teaching and learning have been posited at various times, the overarching image remains of a single instructor standing in front of a classroom and lecturing or otherwise talking to students who are sitting in rows (Barr and Tagg, 1995; Pratt, 1998). The implications are evident about who possesses greater knowledge, and therefore power. The teacher is seen as the dominant force, with students looking up to her or him as the all-knowing expert. This format is accepted, and indeed expected, at many institutions today, though it conflicts with what we know about best practices for teaching and learning.

Approaches to online education, however, tend to derive from constructivist principles of learning in which knowledge is co-created by students and the instructor acts as the facilitator of information (Hanna, 2003; Meyer, 2002). Instructors are then relegated to the role of content expert in course creation, often working with technologists and other specialists to create an interactive environment for students. An instructor is essentially placed in a bifurcated role in which she or he is the content expert in preparing a class and facilitator of information during the class itself. Trends in teaching and learning since Barr and Tagg's (1995) new paradigm for undergraduate instruction also support the need for variety in instructional methodology, in-depth communication with learners, and a greater emphasis on student responsibility for their own learning. Despite the number of books that encourage these more inclusive methods of teaching in an online environment (Bender, 2003; Palloff and Pratt, 2004, 2007), Hanna (2003), in describing the "evolution of teaching and learning" at a distance, pointed out that until recently, instruction at a distance has been the domain of a single instructor imparting information to a student or group of students. Thus, when evaluations of quality are made at the course level, the perception of quality may differ depending on whether traditional or contemporary views of instruction are being used as a frame.

Moving Toward Common Ground

The continuous growth in online courses and programs shows that online education is more than just a passing fad, and as more students and educators turn to online education, we need to find common ground in establishing measures of quality rather than seeking a single means of assessing multiple courses and programs with varying goals. The following questions may be used as a starting point for developing common definitions of quality for an online education program:

- How do you define quality in your courses and programs? Consider existing institutional standards as well as accreditation requirements.
- What elements must be assessed to determine quality? Elements to consider include course design, course content, faculty training, faculty evaluations, programmatic requirements, availability of courses, student services, and technology assistance.
- What means do you use to assess online courses? How can these means be improved or built on?
- What are other institutions doing that you can borrow or adapt?
- How are you sharing quality assessment results with stakeholders?
- Is quality a stated measure of online courses and their unique elements, or is the definition of quality based on outdated ideals?
- How do your stakeholders define quality?
- How are online courses and programs included in long-term strategic planning? How does online education support your institutional mission?

These questions provide a starting point for conversations about quality at the macrolevel. These conversations may lead to policy formation or revision for online programs. Determining which measures of quality are best for a particular college requires generating conversation about teaching, learning, student services, and academic services in both online and on-site locations. Once these conversations are started, mechanisms for assessing the quality of courses and programs should be developed. We often attempt to fit quality into existing measures. I suggest that we first define what we mean by quality at course, program, and institutional levels before developing means to accurately assess if we are meeting the desired standards.

Recommendations for Practice

Many of the current policies and practices in place regarding the quality of online education have been developed as reactionary measures when problems arise. I recommend the following to ensure that quality of online education is assessed appropriately:

1. Start collegewide discussions around the idea of quality.
2. Determine appropriate levels for assessing quality of education at course, program, or department levels.
3. Align the institutional definition of quality with those required by accrediting or other outside agencies.
4. Examine existing measures for their appropriateness in assessing online courses or programs, and adjust accordingly.
5. Assess the assessment measures. Are they telling you what you need to know?

6. Continue to refine and modify assessment systems until you are able to assess quality of online education in accordance with institutionally created definitions.

7. Be open to change. Online education has undergone dramatic transformation in its relatively short existence, and it will undoubtedly continue to evolve. Be sure that determinations of quality continue to evolve with other changes in online education.

References

Barr, R. B., and Tagg, J. "A New Paradigm for Undergraduate Education." *Change, 27* (6), 1995, 13-25.

Bender, T. *Discussion-Based Online Teaching to Enhance Student Learning: Theory, Practice, and Assessment.* Sterling, Va.: Stylus, 2003.

Bourne, J., and Moore, J. C. (eds.). *Elements of Quality Online Education.* Newbury, Mass.: Sloan Center for Online Education, 2001.

Hanna, D. E. "Organizational Models in Higher Education, Past and Future." In M. G. Moore and W. G. Anderson (eds.), *Handbook of Distance Education.* Mahwah, N.J.: Erlbaum, 2003.

Lederman, D. The Challenge of Comparability. *Inside Higher Ed,* Aug. 4, 2009, Retrieved from: http://www.insidehighered.com/news/2009/08/04/transparency.

McDonald, J. "Is 'As Good as Face-to-Face' as Good as It Gets?" *Journal of Asynchronous Learning Networks,* 2002, *6*(2), 10-23. Retrieved Mar. 30, 2008, from http://www.sloan-c.org/publications/jaln/v6n2/v6n2_macdonald.asp.

Meyer, K. A. *Quality in Distance Education: Focus on Online Learning.* ASHE-ERIC Higher Education Report, *29*(4). San Francisco: Jossey-Bass, 2002.

Palloff, R. M., and Pratt, K. *Collaborating Online: Learning Together in Community.* San Francisco: Jossey-Bass, 2004.

Palloff, R. M., and Pratt, K. *Building Online Learning Communities: Effective Strategies for the Virtual Classroom.* (2nd ed.) San Francisco: Jossey-Bass, 2007.

Pratt, D. *Five Perspectives on Teaching in Adult and Higher Education.* Malabar, FL: Krieger, 1998.

Russell, T. L. *The No Significant Difference Phenomenon.* Raleigh, N.C.: North Carolina State University Press, 1999.

Sener, J. "Escaping the Comparison Trap: Evaluating Online Learning on Its Own Terms." *Innovate,* 2004, *1*(2). Retrieved Jan. 17, 2008, from http://innovateonline.info/index.php?view=article&id=11&action=article.

REGINA L. GARZA MITCHELL is assistant professor of educational leadership at Central Michigan University in Mount Pleasant, Michigan. She was previously director of distance education for a medium-sized rural community college.

10

This chapter describes some of the lessons learned during the evolution of distance education and suggests several important elements that practitioners should consider as they strategically plan for the future of online learning.

Teaching the World to Sing: Planning for the Future of Online Learning

Albert L. Lorenzo

A bold new television commercial for Coca-Cola, first aired in the United States in July 1971, featured a large group of young multinational singers standing on a hillside near Rome. The opening line, "I'd like to teach the world to sing," later became the title of a pop song that topped the music charts in both the United States and Europe. Now known as the "hilltop" ad, it appealed artistically to the growing desire for international unity and world peace. Commercially it foretold the emergence of a global market for American consumer goods. But what could not have been anticipated was that a generation later, given access to the appropriate digital and Internet technology, it would literally be possible for a gifted vocalist to teach another person anywhere in the world to sing.

The Internet has expanded the potential for learning exponentially. Its greatest gift has been greater access, and while academics will continue to debate the "equivalency" of online course work, no one can dispute the personal empowerment that has resulted. Much like the goal of the Coke commercial, online learning has become a means for repositioning a traditional product. It has transformed our concept of learning from a collective and place-bound activity to an individual experience set within a global network of students and teachers. For colleges, it has become the ultimate resource for outreach.

Most colleges entered the world of online learning more by happenstance than by design. Initial offerings were typically determined by faculty

New Directions for Community Colleges, no. 150, Summer 2010 © 2010 Wiley Periodicals, Inc.
Published online in Wiley InterScience (www.interscience.wiley.com) • DOI: 10.1002/cc.409

interest or willingness to develop a course rather than as part of a comprehensive plan. Things have improved, but many institutions still find it easier to plan for on-campus programs than for their online counterparts. The purpose of this concluding chapter is to help close that gap by suggesting how community colleges can plan more strategically for online learning. It describes lessons learned from historical and current practices and concludes by suggesting essential elements to consider during the planning process.

Historical Lessons

Although the terms *distance education* and *online learning* are often used interchangeably, the distinction between the two is important. *Distance education* is a term that encompasses a variety of delivery systems employed during the past two centuries to bridge the geographical distance between students and teachers. It has evolved from written correspondence to recordings, from radio to television, and from audiovisual to computer based, and now to the Internet. Strictly speaking, *online learning* describes only the most recent iteration of distance education.

Shared Purposes.   History reminds us that all forms of distance education have shared similar purposes and practices, such as enhancing access, providing greater flexibility, being asynchronous, relying on independent study, and requiring different pedagogy. Campus leaders should continue to keep these characteristics at the center of their planning conversations, and they should guard against becoming preoccupied with the technology. While most colleges have incorporated online learning into their curriculum, the technical aspects of that approach often distract them from addressing issues of content and teaching. The focus of planning should be on the opportunities to be created and the outcomes to be achieved, not the medium to be employed. The technology is important, but learning is the goal.

Life Cycle.   History also reminds us of the importance of understanding product life cycles. Except for correspondence programs, previous distance delivery systems have had relatively short life spans. All technology evolves, with the newest discovery either displacing or completely eliminating what came before. The telephone eliminated the telegraph, and television displaced radio. Planners must think about life cycles even when the technology appears to have long-term potential.

While it is difficult to believe that the Internet will ever be eliminated, its utility could be diminished by some future discovery, and learning management platforms are evolving rapidly. What could possibly displace the use of the Internet for distance learning? Possibilities are interactive holographs, personalized learning devices, and genetic biomedical implants. Because every new discovery will have a useful life, planners must avoid the technology trap by constantly looking beyond current alternatives and making investment and product decisions that align with future life cycle probabilities.

Today's Lessons

The first decade of the new millennium has seen continued double-digit growth in the popularity of Internet-based education. Given current enrollment trends, it is reasonable to expect that more than 4 million college students will take at least one online course during 2009. No previous form of distance education has grown so rapidly or as consistently, and community colleges have been at the vanguard of that transition. While associate degree institutions account for just over a third of all college students, they enroll over half of online students (Allen and Seaman, 2008).

Increasing Demand. A survey released in 2008 by the Instructional Technology Council (Lokken, Womer, and Mullins, 2008) reported an 18 percent increase in distance education enrollments at community colleges, up from a 15 percent increase in the prior year. The council used these findings to suggest that online enrollment has probably not peaked at community colleges. The survey also found that online offerings by community colleges were moving from individual courses toward complete degrees. Sixty-four percent of the responding colleges reported offering at least one online degree, and 70 percent indicated that student demand exceeded their online offerings.

Finding Faculty. The unprecedented demand for online opportunities has brought with it a predictable challenge: finding enough properly prepared faculty to meet the need. Since administrators most often look to the existing campus faculty to develop and teach online courses (Guess, 2008), the vast majority of community colleges have established in-house training programs. By 2008, fully 96 percent of community colleges reported offering specific distance education training for their faculty. But even with the best of efforts, planners should anticipate that the demand for online learning is likely to outpace faculty availability, at least for the foreseeable future.

Continuing Skepticism. Despite record growth rates, faculty training, and preliminary research findings, there is still substantial skepticism about the effectiveness of online learning, especially among faculty at four-year institutions. More than ten thousand faculty members at sixty-seven public four-year campuses responded to a survey regarding online instruction conducted by the National Association of State Universities and Land-Grant Colleges (Shieh, 2009). Although 30 percent felt that online courses provided superior or equivalent learning when compared to face-to-face classes, 70 percent felt that learning outcomes were inferior. That figure dropped to 48 percent for faculty who had taught an online course, but still a majority held a negative view.

Employers are also skeptical, but less so than university faculty. A commissioned study by Zogby International found that 45 percent of more than fifteen hundred chief executive officers surveyed thought online programs were as credible as traditional college campus courses (Tahmincioglu, 2008). But of those familiar with online colleges, 83 percent believed online programs were just as credible. Some of the improvement in employer regard for online learning has been attributed to the growth in the number of well-established schools offering online options.

Since Internet use has experienced an adoption rate unlike any other communication technology, steep demand curves and skepticism are to be expected, especially in early life cycle stages. Both should begin to level off over time, but they still need to be considered in the strategic planning process. Finding an increasingly larger pool of qualified online faculty, however, may likely present an ongoing planning challenge.

Essential Strategic Planning Elements

Anyone who has participated in organizational planning realizes how strongly the past imposes itself on the future. As a result, planning for the future of online learning should begin with a commitment to developing "perfect world" scenarios—those that are unconstrained by current ideology and practice. Feasibility can be assessed later in the process. Defining the perfect world begins by asking what the institution would do or how it would look if it were developed from scratch today. Planners should also predetermine a list of essential elements to be addressed in the planning process. For example, Beaudoin (2003) suggests asking questions about faculty availability, the long-term impact on physical facilities and institutional viability, and growing competition. The balance of this chapter suggests several other elements that community colleges should consider in their strategic planning discussions.

Mission.   An organization's mission clarifies its purposes and legitimizes its actions. So the first strategic questions should be: How important is online learning to our institution's future, and what purposes should it serve? A 2008 survey of online education supported by the Sloan Foundation suggests that the majority of institutions believe online learning is strategically important. Nearly 71 percent of the chief academic officers at public colleges and universities agreed that online education was critical to the long-term strategy of their institutions (Allen and Seaman, 2008). That sentiment is likely to trend upward as student demand increases.

Although there is strong agreement on importance, there may be less clarity regarding purpose. Internet-based education has two broad purposes: to serve as an alternative delivery system and to extend outreach. Converting traditional campus-based curriculum to electronic formats is a market-wise practice and may attract more students, but this is not the same as making an institutional commitment to extend outreach. True outreach means deliberate efforts to serve historically underserved or disenfranchised populations and requires a different approach to both curriculum design and support services.

Markets.   Although the Internet enables community colleges to teach students around the world, the majority of online learners are much closer to home. For example, enrollment summaries complied by the Michigan Community College Association (2008) revealed that less than 5 percent of the more than fifty thousand online course enrollments statewide were at other than the student's home institution. In fact, one Instructional Technology Council board member was quoted in *Inside Higher Ed* as suggesting that the phrase *distance education* should be dropped, since so few community college online students are really learning at a great distance (Jaschik, 2007). So the issue of extending market reach becomes a key strategic question. Just how far beyond its traditional borders does the institution want to venture, and what will be the implications of that decision?

Specialization.   One practical strategy for extending market reach is to target a limited number of specialized or niche programs. Most community colleges have developed on-campus programs that have unique content and faculty expertise or have earned regional or national reputations for excellence. Although there will still be risks, these programs offer the best chance for success in an increasingly competitive online environment. Employer partnerships and contract training are other ways of extending market reach with lessened risk.

Course Mix.   In order to monitor trends in online education, Allen and Seaman (2003) proposed three standard definitions for *Internet-based instruction*. An *online course* has at least 80 percent of its content delivered online and typically does not require face-to-face meetings. A *Web-facilitated course* has less than 30 percent of its content available online and uses the Internet primarily to augment what is essentially a face-to-face course. And a *blended* or *hybrid course* has a substantial portion of the content delivered online while retaining a requirement for some face-to-face meetings. Institutions should monitor their proportions of online delivery and, more important, agree on course mix targets as an outcome of their strategic planning process.

Learner Profiles.   Howell, Williams, and Lindsay (2003) noted that higher education profiles for online, information age, and adult students are changing. They quoted Diaz (2002) who said these students are "generally older, have completed more college credit hours and more degree programs, and have a higher all-college GPA than their traditional counterparts." Community colleges should systematically monitor the academic and demographic profiles of their online learners to see where they differ from traditional student populations. Those differences should be considered in the planning process, especially as they relate to curriculum design, scheduling patterns, and course mix alternatives.

Equity Agenda.   Two cohorts likely to be underrepresented in online learner profiles are low-income and at-risk populations. Whether these individuals lack access to or experience with the technology or fail to possess the study skill typically required for success, their numbers are usually small. Cox (2006) contends that extending geographical access is not the same as increasing educational opportunities, especially for less advantaged students. For these students, online learning must do more than simply create an opportunity to enroll.

Many community colleges have developed an equity agenda by combining their commitment to open access with a strong commitment to equalizing learning outcomes and goal attainment for all students. Part of the planning process should consider whether online learning will be used to support an equity agenda. If it is, then institutions will have to incorporate appropriate curriculum, delivery, and student support strategies into the final plan.

Capacity.   Concerns are often expressed about whether higher education has the capacity to keep up with growing demands and economic challenges. Howell, Williams, and Lindsey (2003) were clear in their belief that the physical higher education infrastructure cannot accommodate growing enrollment demands, thus making distance education programs a necessity. But is there also an upper limit for online learning? If so, to what extent is it determined by controllable factors? To what extent is it a function of the marketplace? Each institution should use these kinds of questions during the planning process to develop some sense of its capacity for online learning. It can then choose to live within that capacity or begin exploring the means to strengthen it.

Structures.   Online learning has moved from ancillary to mainstream at most institutions, yet in many cases, it remains bound by policies, practices, and labor agreements that were designed around traditional delivery systems. A good example is the requirement for purely online faculty to hold on-campus office hours. If community colleges hope for continued growth in online education, their strategic planning process will have to critically examine whether their current structures will support that goal. In many cases, they are likely to conclude that they will not. Changing structures is never easy, and that may be the point in the process where the perfect world begins to give way to reality.

Political Will.   The planning process should conclude with an honest assessment of political will. Progress usually requires change, and change is always challenging. A decade ago, Bates (2000) described some of the barriers to advancing online learning as the lack of faculty interest, the absence of alternative models, and the financial implications for institutions. Bates felt the biggest challenges were the lack of vision and the failure to use technology strategically. Since that time, some of those barriers have been resolved, but others persist. Today, however, the greatest barrier to more fully harnessing the potential of online learning may be quite different.

In their book exploring the condition of American society near the end of the twentieth-century, Cetron and Davies (1989) suggested that virtually all of the major problems facing our society persist not because we lack solutions but because the nation lacks the political will to change in fundamental ways. This may also be an apt description of the mood on many college campuses today, not just about online learning but about many potential advances. The vision is clear, new models have been developed, the technology has been perfected, the research has been done, and the market is ready. What is often missing is the collective will to make the necessary changes.

Conclusion

Despite the rapid growth of online learning, many would argue that it is still in its infancy. If so, community colleges have enormous potential to use this delivery system to advance their historic mission and reach out to students in many new ways. The most difficult strategic question may be whether they can muster the willingness to change as they attempt to teach the world to sing.

References

Allen, I. E., and Seaman, J. *Sizing the Opportunity: The Quality and Extent of Online Education in the United States, 2002 and 2003.* Needham, Mass.: Sloan Consortium, 2003.

Allen, I. E., and Seaman, J. *Staying the Course: Online Education in the United States, 2008.* Needham, Mass.: Sloan Consortium, 2008.

Bates, A. W. "Distance Education in Dual Mode Higher Education Institutions: Challenges and Changes." The Future of Learning. Retrieved July 16, 2000, from http://bates.cstudies.ubc.ca/papers/challengesandchanges.html.

Beaudoin, M. F. "Distance Education Leadership for the New Century." *Online Journal of Distance Learning Administration,* 2003. 6(2). Retrieved July 23, 2009 from http://www.westga.edu/%7Edistance/ojdla/summer62/beaudoin62.html.

Cetron, M., and Davies, O. *American Renaissance: Our Life at the Turn of the 21st Century.* New York: St. Martin's Press, 1989.

Cox, R. D. "Virtual Access." In T. Bailey and V. S. Morest (eds.), *Defending the Community College Equity Agenda.* Baltimore, MD.: Johns Hopkins University Press, 2006.

Diaz, D. P. "Online Drop Rates Revisited." Technology Source, May/June 2002. Retrieved July 23, 2009 from http://technologysource.org/article/online_drop_rates_revisited/.

Guess, A. "With Students Flocking Online, Will Faculty Follow?" *Inside Higher Ed,* Nov. 18, 2008. Retrieved July 23, 2009 from http://www.insidehighered.com/news/2008/11/18/online.

Howell, S. L., Williams, P. B., and Lindsay, N. K. "Thirty-Two Trends Affecting Distance Education: An Informed Foundation for Strategic Planning." *Online Journal of Distance Learning Administration,* 2003 6,(3). Retrieved July 23, 2009 from http://www.westga.edu/%7Edistance/ojdla/fall63/howell63.html.

Jaschik, S. "Surge in Distance Ed at Community Colleges." *Inside Higher Ed,* Apr. 16, 2007. Retrieved July 23, 2009 from http://www.insidehighered.com/news/2007/04/16/aacc.

Lokken, F., Womer, L., and Mullins, C. *2007 Distance Education Survey Results: Tracking the Impact of e-Learning at Community Colleges.* Washington, D.C.: Instructional Technology Council, 2008.

Michigan Community College Association. "MCCVLC Enrollment Report—Fall 2008. Lansing, Mich.: Michigan Community College Association, 2008.

Shieh, D. "Professors Regard Online Instruction as Less Effective Than Classroom Teaching." *Chronicle of Higher Education,* Feb. 10, 2009. Retrieved July 23, 2009 from http://chronicle.com/daily/2009/02/11232n.htm.

Tahmincioglu, E. "Online Degrees Gaining More Respect." MSNBC.com. Sept. 7, 2008, Retrieved July 23, 2009 from http://www.msnbc.msn.com/id/26458424/print/1/displaymode/1098/.

ALBERT L. LORENZO *is president emeritus of Macomb Community College in Warren, Michigan, and is now executive in residence at Oakland University in Rochester, Michigan.*

INDEX

League for Innovation in the Community College, 19

Learning Action Plan: A New Approach to Information Technology Planning in Community Colleges (Baltzer), 19

Learning and course management system (LCMS), 60; adaptability and support considerations, 61*t*

Lederman, D., 91

Lee, J. L., 48

Leist, J., 3, 17

Leithwood, K., 72

Lester, J., 3, 67

Levin, J. S., 45, 47

Lewis, L., 7, 13

Life cycle, 96–97

Lindsay, N. K., 99, 100

Loke, J.C.F., 70

Lokken, F., 8, 9, 11, 12, 14, 97

Lorenzo, A. L., 3, 95

Louisiana, 11

Lowery, J. W., 80

LunarStorm social networking site, 68

Madden, M., 75

Maricopa Community College District (Arizona), 19

Martin, Q., III, 82

Martinez Aleman, A. M., 68, 74

Mastrodicasa, J., 68

Matney, M., 68

Maughan, G. R., 18–20

MCCVLC. *See* Michigan Community College Virtual Learning Collaborative (MCCVLC)

McDonald, J., 90

McLean, M., 79, 86

Meyer, K. A., 1–2, 38, 90, 92

Michigan, 34, 35; community colleges in, 31; loss of population in, 34

Michigan Community College Association, 99

Michigan Community College Virtual Learning Collaborative (MCCVLC), 29–30, 32

Mid Michigan Community College (MMCC), 27–36; Academic Support Center, 29; challenges and opportunities at, 30–32; conclusions and lessons learned at, 34–35; development and implementation of online courses at, 28–30; improvements and benefits at, 32–33; institutional

change at, 33–34; suggestions for practice at, 35–36

Middle Ages, 44

Miller, S. E., 72

Minsun, S., 34

Mixi social networking site, 68

MMCC. *See* Mid Michigan Community College (MMCC)

Moeck, P., 13

Moller, L., 28

Moneta, L., 82

Moore, J. C., 91

Moore, M. G., 2

Mt. Pleasant, Michigan, 28

Muller, T., 31

Mullins, C., 97

Mupinga, D. M., 18–20

Murray, J. P., 18

MySpace, 68

National Association of State Universities and Land-Grant Colleges, 97

National Center for Career and Technical Education (Johnson and Benson), 32

National Center for Education Statistics (NCES), 7, 9

National Study of Student Engagement (NSSE), 74, 81

NCES. *See* National Center for Education Statistics (NCES)

Nelson, M. R., 58

Netvibes, 60

New Mexico, 11

NSSE. *See* National Study of Student Engagement (NSSE)

Ohio Board of Regents of the University System, 34

Oklahoma, 11

Online community college faculty: essential tasks and skills for, 43–54; finding, 97; and online course production model, 50–53; as profession, 44–45; and quality assurance, 64–65; skills for, 48–50; suggestions for practice, 53–54; tasks for, 45–48

Online course production model, 50–53; and collegial production, 51–52; and craft production, 50–51; and rebuilding essential tasks, 52–53; and virtual assembly line production, 52

LB2328 N48 no.150

Online education